EARLY CHURCH RECORDS

OF

ROCKINGHAM COUNTY
VIRGINIA

F. Edward Wright

HERITAGE BOOKS
2025

HERITAGE BOOKS

AN IMPRINT OF HERITAGE BOOKS, INC.

Books, CDs, and more—Worldwide

For our listing of thousands of titles see our website
at
www.HeritageBooks.com

A Facsimile Reprint
Published 2025 by
HERITAGE BOOKS, INC.
Publishing Division
5810 Ruatan Street
Berwyn Heights, MD 20740

International Standard Book Number
Paperbound: 978-1-58549-161-2

CONTENTS
of
Early Church Records of Rockingham County, Virginia

INTRODUCTION[1]

Rockingham County was formed out of Augusta County in 1778. This book consists of all the church records available for this region prior to the 19th century, beginning in the mid 1750s.

Röder's Church may have been formed in the 1740s, definitely by 20 May 1765 the date of a deed which refers to a union church. Charles H. Glatfelter states that the earliest Lutheran register begins in 1772 and the Reformed register in 1787.

Peaked Mountain Church (Upper Peaked Mountain, Stony Creek) was organized before 1760. Glatfelter lists the following Lutheran ministers: George Samuel Klug, Henry Wortmann (1757-1758), John Schwarbach (1765-1775), Jacob Frank (1775-1776), Michael Schmidt (1782-1785), Abraham Deschler (1785), Christian Streit (1788), William Carpenter (1789), and Peter Ahl (1792-1796). The Reformed ministers included Philip Van Gemuenden (1762-1764), William Hendel (1766), Charles Lange (1768), Henry Giese (1786), William Runkel (1786), Jacob Weymer (1786-1789), and Bernard Willy.

Friedens Church was formed as a union church (Lutheran and Reformed) by the early 1760s. Lutheran ministers were as follows: Abraham Deschler (1786), George Butler, Peter Ahl (c.1792-1796), and Adolph Spindler.

St. Michael's may have been formed in 1764 as a union church. Benjamin Henkel served the Lutheran congregation at the time of his death in 1792. Bernard Willy served the Reformed in the late 1780s and early 1790s. The Lutheran congregation had left the church by 1803.

Trinity Lutheran Church may have been founded about 1787, the year Abraham Deschler was pastor. The register begins in 1798. Originally it was called Ermentraut's or Armentrout's Church.

Smith's and Linville's Creek Baptist Church met alternately on Smith's Creek and Linville's Creek. In 1774 Smith's Creek Church was constituted as an independent congregation. Linville's Creek Baptist Church continued. Abstracts of the minutes of both congregations are given in this work. For more detailed abstracts of the minutes of Smith's and Linville's Creek Church see Virginia Valley Records.

John Alderson was pastor at Linville's Creek Baptist Church. Marriages performed by him are shown on pages 73-90. Photostat copies of the originals are difficult to read; interpretations of the names shown in these records vary in their publication in William and Mary Quarterly and in Virginia Valley Records. Comparisons are made in this work.

F. Edward Wright
Westminster, Maryland
1998

[1] Much of the information on the Lutheran and Reformed Church records was taken from Charles H. Glatfelter, Pastors and People Volume I. Pastors and Congregations. 1980.

BIBLIOGRAPHY

Clark, Jewell T. and Elizabeth Terry Long. A Guide to Church Records in the Archives Branch Virginia State Library and Archives. 1981.

Glatfelter, Charles H. Pastors and People Volume I. Pastors and Congregations. 1980.

Hinke, William J. and Charles E. Kemper, William and Mary Quarterly, series 1, 13 (1904-1905): 247-256, and 14 (1905-1906): 9-19, 186-193.

Stirewalt, Jerome P. A Brief History of Rader's Lutheran Church ... 1765-1921. 1922.

Wayland, John W. Virginia Valley Records. 1930.

RöDER'S CHURCH

Translated by Rodger Bundy

Röder's Church, Rockingham County, Va. 1st January 1787
This Church protocol includes births and baptisms under the
inspection and overview of the Reverend Pastor Paulus Hinckle and
of the current worthy church council made up of elders and
directors.

Elders:	Andreas Zerckel
	Casper Brenner
Representatives:	Christmann Bob
	Johannes Roller
Secretary:	P. Weber, Schoolmaster.

1) Salome Bün of Johannes Bün & Elisabeth, b. March 1790, bapt.
Easter Monday 1791, spon. Adreas Andes & his wife Barbara.
Scriptum pena ligne [from latin:written with pen and writing
tablet]

Written by another hand.
2) May 18, 1796 - Elisabetha.

A son of Johannes Gerblinger & Elisabetha, b. Feb 15, 1796, bapt.
Aug 1796, spon: Heinrich Schumacher & Elisabetha.
A baby girl of Matheus Will, b. Jul 14, 1796, spon: Catherina Zeblen.
Magdelena Zerkel of Micheal Zerkel, Junior & Elisabetha, b. Aug
11, 1786, bapt. Dec 31, 1786, spon: Andreas & Catherina Zerkel.
Elisabetha Zerkel of Micheal Zerkel, Junior & Elisabetha, b. May
28, 1788, bapt. Sep 14, 1788, spon: Christian & Elisabeth
Eberhardt.

1) Sara Brenner of John Brenner & Catherine, b. Jan 20, 1786, bapt.
Jul 31, 1787, spon: Caspar & Catherina Brenner.
2) Casper Brenner of Johannes Brenner and Catherina, b. Feb 25,
1794, bapt. 1774, spon: Casper Brenner, [who was?] bapt. 1774
3) Philip, b. Apr 15, 1775, bapt. 1775, spon: Philip Herbein & wife.
4) Maria Magdelena, b. Dec 19, 1776, bapt. in same year.
5) Christina, b. Apr 3, 1778, spon: Casper Brenner.
6) Maria, b. Dec 23, 1779, spon: Magdalena Herpin.
7) Catherina, b. Jul 29, 1781, spon: Catherina Brenner.

8) Sarah, b. Jun 20, 1786, bapt. Jul 31, 1787, spon: Casper Brenner.
9) Johannes, b. May 29, 1791, bapt. Jun 11, 1791. Spon: parents.
Maria Röder of Michael Röader(Röder) & Catherina, b. Feb 18,
    1786, bapt. Apr 17, 1786, spon: Andreas & Maria Catherina
    Zerkel.
(Wilhelm)? [sic] Röder of Michael Röder & Catherina, b. Mar 26
    1784, bapt. May 9, 1784, spon: parents.
Michael Röder of Michael Röder & Catherina, b. Feb 12, 1788, bapt.
    Apr 13, 1788, spon: Johannes Neehs & Elisabetha
Johannes Röder of Adam Röder & Clara, b. Jan 11, 1784, bapt. Sep
    8, 1787, spon: Michael & Catherina Röder.
Ambrosius Hinckel of Wilhelm Röther & wife, b. Feb 28, 1832, bapt.
    May 1, 1834, in the parsonage, spon: parents.
Ambrosius Hinckel of Wilhelm Röther & wife, b. Aug 30, 1833, spon:
    Robert Cogli & wife.
Magdelena Peter of Abraham & Catherina Peter, b. May 24, 1787,
    bapt. Aug 26, 1787, spon: parents.
Catherina Peter of Abraham & Catherina Peter, b. Jul 1, 1789, bapt.
    Nov 22, 1789, spon: Georg & Magdalena Huf.

Page 4 General Record
Abraham Petter Jr. of (Abraham Petter Sr. & wife), b. Dec 11, 1791,
    bapt. May 13, 1792, spon: Abraham Petter Sr. & wife.
Maria Hautemeyer of Jacob & Dorothea Hautemeyer, b. Jan 13,
    1786, spon: John & Anna Roller
Johannes Christian Hautemeyer of Jacob & Dorothea Hautemeyer,
    b. Feb 23, 1784, bapt. May 30, 1784, spon: parents.
Georg Wagner of Jacob & Elisabetha Wagner, b. Mar 30, 1786, bapt.
    Jun 26, 1786, spon: Conrad & Hanna Seybel.
Andreas Orbach of Andreas & Margaretha Orbach, b. Apr 21, 1786,
    bapt. Jun 26, 1786, spon: Andreas & Barbara Anters.
Sussana Orbach of Andreas & Margaretha Orbach, b. Sep 24, 1783,
    bapt. Oct 25, 1784, spon: Johannes & Barbara Anters [based on
    possible ditto].
Johann Ernst Kühl of Conrad & Catherina Kühl, b. Mar 3, 1786,
    bapt. Apr 26, 1786, spon: Adam & Elisabetha Haberstick.
Margaretha Eder of Heinrich & Magdalena Eder, b. Jan 15, 1786,
    bapt. Jun 27, 1786, spon: Heinrich & Margaretha Neef.
A daughter of Heinrich & Magdalena Eder, b. Dec 1783, bapt. May
    9, 1784, spon: Johannes & Appollonia Krehterich.

Rahel Berret of Joseph & Anna Maria Berret, b. Dec 9, 1785, bapt. Jun 26, 1786, spon: parents.

Heinrich Traut of Georg Michael & Elisabetha Traut, b. Mar 10, 1786, bapt. Jan 26, 1786, spon: parents.

Johannes Traut of Georg Michael & Elisabetha Traut, b. Jan 1, 1784, bapt. Sep 3, 1786, spon: parents.

Maria Traut of Georg Michael & Elisabetha Traut, b. Oct 2, 1788, bapt. Apr 5, 1789, spon: parents.

A daughter of Georg Michael & Elisabetha Traut, b. Feb 9, 1791, bapt. May 156, 1791.

Noa Walther of Thomas & Elisabetha Walther, b. Dec 16, 1785, bapt. Feb 16, 1786, spon: Widow Catherina Syvel(in)

A daughter of Heinrich Schmacher & wife, b. Nov 15, 1783, bapt. May 9, 1784, spon: Joseaff & Anna Perel.

A son of Heinrich Schumacher & wife, b. Sep 15, 1818?, bapt. Jun 5, 1819, spon: parents.

Lianna Schumacher, a son of Heinrich Schumacher & wife, b. Nov 1820, bapt. Oct 28, 1821.

Anna Münch of Johannes & Elisabetha Münch, b. Mar 31, 1786, bapt. Aug 27, 1786, spon: Mart & Catherina Zeifas.

A child of Johannes & Elisabetha Münch, b. Apr 5, 1784, bapt. May 9, 1784, spon: Johannes & Appollonis Küstric

A daughter of Jacob & Magdalena Maas, b. Sep 16, 1782, bapt. May 30, 1784, spon: Georg & Catherina Springer.

A son of Jacob & Magdalena Maas, b. Dec 1, 1783, bapt. May 30, 1784, spon: Georg & Catherina Springer.

Johannes Jacob Maas of Jacob & Magdalena Maas, b. Oct 9, 1785, bapt. Aug 29, 1785, spon: Georg & Catherina Springer.

Johannes Maas of Jacob & Magdalena Maas, b. Jun 1, 1788, bapt. Jun 29, 1788, spon: parents.

Johannes Heinrich Maas of Jacob & Magdalena Maas, b. Jun 24, 1790, bapt. Jun 14, 1791, spon: parents.

Abraham Rübel of Georg & Catherina Rübel, b. Dec 22, 1784, bapt. Sep 3, 1785, spon: Michael & Magdalena Zahm.

Catherina Zahm of Michael & Magdalena Zahm, b. Sep 11, 1784, bapt. Jun 3, 1784, spon: Georg & Catherina Rübel.

Georg Tolt of Johannes & Eva Tolt, b. Sep 19, 1785, bapt. Apr 15, 1786, spon: parents.

Sussana Zerckel of Georg Adam & Elisabetha Zerckel, b. Feb 27, 1786, bapt. Aug 27, 1786, spon: parents.

Rosina Zerckel of Georg Adam & Elisabetha Zerckel, b. Jun 28, 1791, bapt. Mar 30, spon: Pastor Hinckel and his wife Elisabetha

Ludwig Zerckel of Ludwig & Maria Magdalena Zerckel, b. Feb 3, 1786, bapt. Apr 15, 1786, spon: Michael Sr. & Catherina Zerckel.

Rahel Zerckel of Ludwig & Maria Magdalena Zerckel, b. Jul 25, 1788, bapt. Sep 14, 1788, spon: Georg & Anna Maria Esterle.

Daniel Zerckel of Ludwig & Maria Magdalena Zerckel, b. Sep 26, 1790, bapt. Apr 22, 1791, spon: Johannes Nes & wife.

A son of Martin & Catherina Zerfas, b. Sep 15, 1783, bapt. Oct 25, 1783, spon: Johannes Bauman.

Anna Catherina Zerfas of Martin & Catherina Zerfas, b. Dec 1, 1785, bapt. Jan 22, 1786, spon: Johannes & Anna Catherina Roller.

Susanna Zerfas of Martin & Catherina Zerfas, b. Aug 28, 1787, bapt. Jan 27, 1788, spon: Susan Münch (single).

Noah Traut of Valentin & Margaretha Traut, b. Jan 31, 1784, bapt. Apr 7, 1784.

Magdalena Traut of Valentin & Margaretha Traut, b. Feb 15, 1786, bapt. Apr 30, 1786, spon: Johannes & Maria Stalp.

Elisabetha Traut of Valentin & Margaretha Traut, b. Dec 11, 1787, bapt. Jun 29, 1788, spon: Michael & Elisabetha Traut.

Eliner Zirckel of Johannes & Eliner Zirckel, b. Jun 13, 1771, bapt. Apr 12, 1789, spon: Ludwig & Magdalena Zirckel.

Maria Magdalena Zirckel of Johannes & Eliner Zirckel, b. Feb 1789, bapt. Apr 12, 1789, spon: Ludwig & Magdalena Zirckel.

1) Lydia (Lidia) Herbein of Abraham & Elisabetha Herbein, b. Apr 13 (General Record) or May 13 (Hinckel Record), bapt. Aug 27, 1786, spon: parents.
2) Catherina Herbein of Abraham & Elisabetha Zirckel, b. Apr 20, 1791, bapt. Jul 24, 1791, spon: Catherina Brenner, the childs grandmother.

Christian Bender of Christian & Maria Bender, b. Jul 18, 1784, bapt. Sep 29, 1784, spon: Philip and Catherina Herbein.

Catherina Bender of Christian & Maria Bender, b. Jun 31, 1787, bapt. May 28, 1787, spon: Jacob and Rahel Perret.

Absalom & Mercy Bender of Christian & Maria Bender, b. Jun 31, 1790, bapt. May 3, 1790, spon: Christian Bender himself and Elisabetha Hinckle, the pastor's wife.

A daughter of Philip & Barbara Henckel, b. Oct 2, 1784, bapt. Feb

26, 1785, spon: Ludwig Volmer.
Catherina Neff of Georg & Veronica Neff, b. Feb 21, 1785, bapt. May
  1, 1785, spon: Johannes & Appolonia Knestrich.
Georg Heim of Johannes & Salome Heim, b. Feb 20, 1785, bapt.
  May 1, 1785, spon: Jacob & Catherina Ketner?
Margaretha Lehr of Ferdinand & Susanna Lehr, b. Jul 28, 1783,
  bapt. Mar 28, 1784, spon: Matheus & Elisabetha Lehr.
Maria Kips of Michael & Catherina Kips, b. Sep 27, 1783, bapt. Apr
  4, 1784.
Johannes Kips of Michael & Catherina Kips, b. Apr 27, 1786, bapt.
  Aug 27, 1786, spon: Johannes & Maria Stalp.
Sara Kips of Michael & Catherina Kips, b. Jul 27, 1789, bapt. May 9,
  1790.
Maria Elisabetha Kips of Michael & Catherina Kips, b. Feb 20,
  1793, spon: Margaretha ----?.
Catherina Kips of Michael & Catherina Kips, b. Mar 12, 1797, bapt.
  Oct 7, 1797, spon: Johannes & Catherina Roller.
Margaretha Kips of Michael & Catherina Kips, b. Mar 19, 1801,
  bapt. May 24, 1801, spon: Widow Elisabetha Ehrhardt.
Hanna Gibs of Michael Gibs, b. 8 Jan 04, 1804, bapt. May 6, 1804,
  spon: Valentin & Christina Poland?
Maria Keltner of Jacob & Catherina Keltner, b. Jul 27, 1783, bapt.
  Apr 4, 1784.
Elisabetha Selzer of Jacob & Catherina Selzer, b. Aug 22, 1786,
  bapt. Jul 28, 1787, spon: Heinrich & Catherina Gut
Catherina Selzer of Jacob & Catherina Selzer, b. Aug 15, 1789, bapt.
  Oct 7, 1790.
Georg Kups of Jacob & Elisabeth Kups, b. Feb 14, 1787, bapt. Jul
  29, 1787, spon: Georg Adam Henckel & wife.
Michael Kups of Jacob & Elisabeth Kups, b. Mar 3, 1789, bapt. Jul
  19, 1789, spon: parents.
Sara Kips of Michael & Catherina Kips, b. Jul 7, 1789, bapt. May 9,
  1790, spon: Michael Kips & wife.
Anna Maria Schmidt of Peter & Anna Maria Schmidt, b. Jun 2,
  1789, bapt. Aug 30, 1789, spon: parents.
Susana Catherina Schmidt of Peter & Anna Maria Schmidt, b. Jan
  23, 1792, bapt. May 13, 1792, spon: Johannes Rohler & wife.
Anna Maria Ehrhardt of Christian & Elisabetha Ehrhardt, b. Aug
  31, 1789, bapt. Oct 25, 1789, spon: Andreas & Catherina Zerckel.
Michael Wolff of Georg & Veronica Wolff, b. Feb 17, 1790, bapt. Apr
  4, 1790, spon: Michael & Catherina Reader.
Michael Ecker of Jacob & Susanna Ecker, b. Apr 22, 1790, bapt.
  May 29, 1790, spon: parents.
Michael Kern of Nicolaus & Elisabetha Kern, b. Apr 28, 1790, bapt.

Aug 22, 1790, spon: parents.

Sara Grim of Johannes & Juliana, b. Jun 12, 1790, bapt. May 23, 1790, spon: Peter Grim & wife.

Sebastian Mortz of Johannes Mortz & wife, b. May 20, 1791, bapt. Oct 9, 1791, spon: the wife.

Maria Elisabeth Sprenger of Georg Sprenger, b. Dec 17, 1790, bapt. Oct 9, 1791, spon: Master Ehrhardt & wife Elisabeth.

Johannes Ehrhardt of Johannes & Margaretha Ehrhardt, b. Sep 24, 1791, bapt. Apr 15, 1792, spon: Christian & Elisabeth Ehrhardt.

Sara Bayr of Peter & Elisabetha Bayr, b. Aug 14, 1790, bapt. 3rd Sunday in Lent, 1791, spon: Jacob & Dorothea Stautermair.

Peter Koch of Johannes & Elisabeth Koch, b. Feb 24, 1762.

Johannes Wilhelm Koch of Johannes & Elisabeth Koch, b. Aug 22, 1763.

Michael Koch of Johannes & Elisabeth Koch, b. Feb 9, 1765.

Susana Koch of Johannes & Elisabeth Koch, b. Jan 12, 1767.

Maria Catherina Koch of Johannes & Elisabeth Koch, b. Jul 23, 1769.

Georg Koch of Johannes & Elisabeth Koch, b. Sep 5, 1771.

Rudolph Koch of Johannes & Elisabeth Koch, b. 24 Jul, 1773.

Elisabetha Koch of Johannes & Elisabeth Koch, b. Feb 23, 1775.

Thomas Koch of Johannes & Elisabeth Koch, b. Oct 24, 1776.

Magdalena Koch of Johannes & Elisabeth Koch, b. Feb 24, 1778.

Philipus Koch of Johannes & Elisabeth Koch, b. Sep 17, 1781.

Adam Koch of Johannes & Elisabeth Koch, b. Jan 6, 1783.

Jacob Koch of Johannes & Elisabeth Koch, b. May 21, 1787, bapt. Jul 22, 1787.

Casper Esterle of Georg & Anna Maria Esterle, b. Nov 24, 1783, bapt. the first day of Christmas 1783, spon: Casper Brenner.

Moses Esterle of Georg & Anna Maria Esterle, b. Nov 12, 1787, bapt. May 12, 1788, spon: parents.

Catherina Esterle of Georg & Anna Maria Esterle, b. Nov 10, 1789, bapt. in the same year, spon: parents.

Magdalena Esterle of Georg & Anna Maria Esterle, b. Jul 4, 1796, spon: parents.

Michael May of Thomas & Catherina May, b. Mar 7, 1790, bapt. May 9, 1790, spon: [indistinct]

Rahel Roller of Johannes & Anna Roller, b. Nov 8, 1783, bapt. 1st
day of Christmas, 1783, spon: Caspar & Catherina Brönner.
Lea Roller of Johannes & Anna Roller, b. Nov 8, 1783, bapt. 1st day
of Christmas, 1783, spon: Johannes & Magdalena Bauman.
Paul Roller of Johannes & Anna Roller, b. Dec, 1786, spon: Pastor
Hinckel & wife Elisabetha
Andreas Roller of Johannes & Anna Roller, b. Dec, 1786, spon:
Georg & Maria Esterle.
Georg Roller of Johannes & Anna Roller, b. Oct 9, 1788, bapt. Dec 7,
1788, spon: Georg & Maria Esterle.
Margaretha Roller of Johannes & Anna Roller, b. Dec 16, 1789,
bapt. Apr 4, 1790, spon: Margaretha Stautermeyer - Johannes
Huber's wife Sarah Roller of Johannes & Anna Roller, b. Mar 7,
1792, bapt. Mar 13, 1792, spon: Jacob & Dorothea Stautermeyer.
Michael Roller of Johannes & Anna Roller, b. Feb 15, 1795, spon:
Michael & Catherina Keipf.
David Roller of Johannes & Catherina Roller, b. May 4, 1798, bapt.
Jun 24, 1798, spon: Andreas & Barbara Andes.
Petrus Roller of Johannes & Catherina Roller, b. Apr 3, 1804, spon:
Michael & Catherina Gibs.
Michael Zirckel of Andreas & Catherina Zirckel, b. Oct 22, 1764,
bapt. in the same year, spon: Michael & Margaretha Ness.
Adam Zirckel of Andreas & Catherina Zirckel, b. Feb 2, 1767, bapt.
in the same year, spon: Casper & Catherina Brenner.
Elisabetha Zirckel of Andreas & Catherina Zirckel, b. Oct 3, 1770,
bapt. in month of Nov, spon: Michael & Catherina Henckel.
Eva Zirckel of Andreas & Catherina Zirckel, b. Jan 17, 1777, bapt.
in Feb, spon: Johannes & Dorothea Rausch.
Andreas Zirckel of Andreas & Catherina Zirckel, b. Oct 11, 1779,
bapt. in the same year, spon: Johannes & Elisabetha Ness.
Johannes Zirckel of Andreas & Catherina Zirckel, b. Mar 21, 1783,
bapt. in the same year, spon: Georg & Catherina Rausch.
Andreas Gäncke, b. Aug 29, 1775, spon: Andreas Zirckel & wife.
Jacob Jancke, b. Aug 29(?), 1775, spon: Jacob & Barbara Mayer.
Anna Bauman of Gottfried & Catherina Bauman, b. Feb 17, 1785,
bapt the 1st day of Pentecost, 1785, spon: parents.
Georg Bauman of Gottfried & Catherina Bauman, b. Jul 7, 1778,
spon: parents.
Johannes Eckart of Jacob & Susanna Eckart, b. Nov 17, 1783, bapt.
Feb 23, 1788, spon: parents.

Adam Eckart of Jacob & Susanna Eckart, b. Sep 1, 1786, bapt. Feb 3, 1788, spon: parents (Adam (youngest) & Johannes were bapt. together).

Johannes Jacob Springer of Georg & Catherina Springer, b. Mar 30, 1788, bapt. Jun 29, 1788, spon: Heinrich Gut.

Georg Springer of Georg & Catherina Springer, b. Nov 3, 1789, bapt. Apr 4, 1790, spon: the father.

A child of Georg & Catherina Springer, b. Feb 5, 1793, spon: Elisabetha Ehrhard(in).

Heinrich Springer of Georg Springer & wife, b. Mar 2, 1795, bapt. Oct 17, 1795, spon: Heinrich Guth & wife - ...? there is no ...?

Magdalena Springer of Georg Springer & wife, b. Jan 29, 1797, bapt. 1st Sunday, 1798, spon: parents.

Johannes Huf of Georg & Magdalena Huf, b. Apr 9, 1788, bapt. Sep 15, 1788, spon: Johannes Huf.

Magdalena Krahn of Friedrich Krahn, b. Nov 21, 1787, bapt. Feb 28, 1788, spon: the mother.

Catherina Krahn of Friedrich Krahn, b. Sep 15, 1789, bapt. Oct 7, 1790, spon: Philip & Catherina Reimel.

Heinrich Heim of Georg & Maria Elisabeth Heim, b. Jan 10, 1789, bapt. Mar 22, 1789, spon: Heinrich & Catherina Baer.

Catherina Baer of Johannes & Elisabeth Baer, b. Nov 28, 1788, bapt. Mar 22, 1789, spon: Heinrich & Catherina Baer & Heinrich's brother.

Magdalena Baer of Johannes & Elisabeth Baer, b. Aug 3, 1800, bapt. Oct 26, 1800, spon: Magdalena Bender.

Heinrich Ewi of Peter & Anna Ewi, b. Mar 4, 1789, bapt. Apr 26, 1789.

Margaretha Ewi of Peter & Anna Ewi, b. Aug, 1792, bapt. Sep 30, 1792, spon: parents.

Anna Maria Ewi of Peter & Anna Ewi, b. Feb 11, 1796, bapt. Jul 10, 1796, spon: Peter & Anna Maria Schmidt.

Magdalena Bauman of Johannes & Magdalen Bauman, b. May 5, 1789, bapt. Jul 5, 1789, spon: parents.

Sara Reinhardt of Adam & Magdalena Reinhardt, b. Jun 11, 1791, bapt. Jul 24, 1791, spon: her grandmother Catherina Brenner.

Adam Olinger of Jacob & Magdalena Olinger, b. Jun 14, 1787, bapt. Mar 30, 1791, spon: parents.

A son of Michael & Catherina Rup, b. Aug 3, 1789, bapt. Mar 30, 1791, spon: parents.

1) Casper Brenner of Michael & Christina Brenner, b. May 22, 1788, bapt. Oct 16, 1791, spon: the grandparents Casper & Catherina Brenner.

2) Catherina Brenner of Michael & Christina Brenner, b. 1791, bapt. Oct 16, 1791, spon: the grandparents Casper & Catherina Brenner.

Eddinus Kempfer of Johannes & Susanna Kempfer, b. 1792, bapt. May 13, 1792, spon: parents.

Catherina Gut of Jacob & Margaretha Gut, b. Feb 1, 1794, bapt. May 17, 1794, spon: parents.

Daniel Gut of Jacob & Margaretha Gut, b. Jul 25, 1795, bapt. Nov 7, 1795, spon: parents.

At end of Hinckel Record Book are some Communicant lists of which the following are the earliest.

June 29, 1788
1. Casper Brenner & wife Catherina
2. Georg Esterle
3. Johannes Koch
4. Andreas Orbach
5. Jacob Guth & wife Margaretha
6. Johannes Roller wife Catherina
7. Andreas Zerckel
8. Maria Braun(in)
9. Johannes Münch wife Elisabeth
10. Jacob Maass & wife Magdalena

Confirmed on Apr 10, 1
1. Valentin Trout
2. Jacob Guth
3. Christian Ehrhardt
4. Philip Guth
5. Jacob Kipf

1. Catherina Neef
2. Christina Zerckel
3. Magdalena Stauterm
4. Elisabetha Kipff
5. Elisabetha Herbein

In the communicant list of May 15, 1791, are these additional names:
1. Johannes Bauman
2. & wife
3. Jacob Keltner
4. & wife
5. Heinrich Guth
6. Christman Pob
7. & wife
8. Peter Sauerwein
9. Peter Koch
10. Johannes Jost Tribi
11. Michael Koch
12. Ludwig Hinckel
13. & wife
14. Friedrich Schäffer
15. & wife
16. Mathaus Hahn
17. Jacob Mussel
18. Georg Springer

19. & wife
20. Johannes Cämphes
21. Margaretha Neff(in)
22. Magdalena Braun(in)
23. Susannah Koch(in)
24. Eva Roller(in)
25. Ludwig Vollmer

26. & wife
27. Margaretha Neff(in)
28. Elisabeth Kipf
29. Christina Kupp
30. Margaretha Lora
31. Master Brenner's wife
32. Catherina Selzer(in), widow

NOTE: Mr. Georg Esterle was installed as director by the Reverend Pastor Paulus Hinckle and ordained by the congregation on 29 June 1788.

1) Salome Andes of Peter & Magdalena Andes, b. Dec 2, 1789, bapt. Aug 21, 1791, spon: Margaretha Kunstseich (single).
2) Elisabeth Andes of Peter & Magdalena Andes, b. Jun 20, 1791, bapt. Aug 21, 1791, spon: Heinrich & Magdalen Eden.
3) Solomon Andes of Peter & Magdalena Andes, b. May 26, 1793, spon: Peter & Maria Sauerwein.
4) Johannes Andes of Peter & Magdalena Andes, b. Nov 26, 1797, spon: Heinrich and Christina Ehly.
5) Abigail Andes of Peter & Magdalena Andes, b. Jun 8, 1800, bapt. May 24, 1801, spon: Johannes & Eva Leibig.

RECORDS OF PEAKED MOUNTAIN CHURCH

BAPTISMS

Michael William Wilhelm of Henry and Anna Elisabeth, b. June 25, 1745; bapt. December 20. Spon: Michael Bauer (Bowers) and wife Catharine.

George Henry William Wilhelm of Henry and Anna Elisabeth, b. April 8, 1747; bapt. July 21. Spon: John George Scherp and wife Marie.

Susanna Preiss (Price) of Augustin and Anna Elisabeth, nee Scherp, b. May 9, 1750; bapt. August 15, 1753. Spon: John Ernst Scherp and wife Anna Margaret.

Conrad Preiss (Price) of Augustin and Anna Elisabeth, nee Scherp, b. December 24, 1752; bapt. August 15, 1753. Spon: Conrad Wahl and Christina Herman.

Augustin Preiss (Price) of Augustin and Anna Elisabeth, nee Scherp, b. December 24, 1754; bapt. October 1, 1756. Spon: Matthew Kirsch (Kersh) and wife Anna Margaret.

Elisabeth Preiss (Price) of Augustin and Anna Elisabeth, nee Scherp, b. September 8, 1757; bapt. October 15. Spon: Parents.

John Frederick Preiss (Price) of Augustin and Anna Elisabeth, nee Scherp, b. September 24, 1759; bapt. October 16. Spon: Frederick Ermentraut and wife Catharine.

Anna Catharine Preiss (Price) of Augustin and Anna Elisabeth, nee Scherp, b. May 4, 1763; bapt. June 19, 1763. Spon: Daniel Preiss and wife Anna Catharine.

Maria Catharine Preiss (Price) of Augustin and Anna Elisabeth, nee Scherp, b. May 12, 1765; bapt. June 18. Spon: Frederick Ermentraut and wife Catharine.

George Valentin Metzger of Valentine and Anna Elisabeth, b. January 21, 1762; bapt. March 2. Spon: Charles Risch (Rush) and wife Maria Elisabeth.

Elisabeth Ermentraut (Armentrout) of Christopher and Susanna, b. February 20, 1761; bapt. March 4. Spon: Elisabeth Ermentraut.

Anna Maria Ermentraut (Armentrout) of Christopher and Susanna, b. February 16, 1762; bapt. March 7. Spon: Anna Maria Gallet.

John Frederick Ermentraut of George and Barbara, b. December --, 1764; bapt. February 10. Spon: John Frederick Ermentraut.

Catharine Barbara Ermentraut of George and Barbara, b. July 24,

1769; bapt. August 13. Spon: John Ermentraut and Barbara Miller.

Henry David Preiss (Price) of Henry and Magdalene, b. March 14, 1759; bapt. June 5. Spon: Henry Ermentraut and wife Magdalene.

Adam Preiss (Price) of Henry and Magdalene, b. July 10, 1760; bapt. July 16. Spon: George Adam Mann and Elisabeth Hermann.

Jacob Nicolaus of John and Margaret, nee Lorentz, b. July 15, 1724; bapt. --. Spon: Jacob Betsch.

Jacob Nicolaus (Nicholas) m. Barbara Zeller, dau. of Henry Zeller (Sellers), on December 7, 1752. They had the following children:

A son, b. July 20, 1753; d. July 29 without bapt. for want of a minister.

Anna Maria, b. September 8, 1754. Spon: Henry Zeller and wife Anna Maria.

John, b. February 6, 1756. Spon: John Zeller, son of Henry Zeller.

John Henry, b. December 6, 1757. Spon: John Henry Zeller and wife Anna Maria.

Anna Catharine, b. February 29, 1760. Spon: Anna Catharine Preiss, wife of Daniel Preiss.

Peter, b. April 5, 1762. Spon: Peter Mueller (Miller) and wife Anna Maria.

Susanna, b. January 25, 1764. Spon: Jacob Argebrecht (Argenbright) and his wife.

Anna Barbara, b. April 22, 1766. Spon: Henry Zeller and his wife.

Elisabeth, b. February 9, 1769. Spon: John Zeller and his wife.

Jacob, b. December 1, 1769. Spon: Peter Mueller and his wife.

Margaret, b. January 1, 1772. Spon: Peter Mueller and his wife.

Anna Elisabeth, b. January 4, 1774. Spon: Anna Elisabeth R(isch).

Sarah Vogt of John Caspar and Elisabeth, b. November 28, 1761; bapt. March 7. Spon: Peter Funck (Funk) and wife Catharine and daughter Margaret.

Elisabeth Hermann (Harman) of Peter and Margaret, nee Choulyn?, b. May 6, 1763. Spon: George Adam Mann and wife Maria Elisabeth.

Philippina Hermann (Harman) of Peter and Margaret, nee Choulyn?, b. ---. Spon: Theobald Hermann and wife Sarah.

George Charles Hermann (Harman) of Peter and Margaret, nee

Choulyn?, b. December 11, 1761; bapt. March 6, 1762. Spon:
George Bernhard Mann and wife Anna Margaret.
Maria Elisabeth Hermann (Harman) of Peter and Margaret, nee
Choulyn?, b. May 6, 1763; bapt. June 17, 1763. Spon: George
Adam Mann and wife Elisabeth.

1762. At the "Pinquit" (Peaked) Mountain and the South
"Chanithor" (Shenandoah), in Virginia, the following children
were baptized on Saturday, February 27th:
Jacob Kropf (Cropp) of Christian and Rosina, nee Kipp, age 26
years. Spon: John Jacob Nicolaus and wife Anna Barbara.
Daniel Kropf (Cropp) of Christian and Rosina, nee Kipp, age 24
years. Spon: Jacob Arkebrecht (Argenbright) and wife Susanna.
Margaret Kropf (Cropp) of Christian and Rosina, nee Kipp, age 18
years. Spon: I. C. Van Genuenden, the Reformed minister at
this place, and wife M. A. Van Gemuenden, also Jacob
Perschinger, Reformed elder, and wife Maria Catharine.

John Jacob Friedel (Fridle) of Ludwig and Margaret, bapt. April 24.
Spon: John Jacob Mann and wife Barbara.
Peter Nicolaus of John Jacob and Barbara, nee Zeller, b. April 5,
1762; bapt. April 25, 1762. Spon: Peter Mueller (Miller) and wife
Maria Margaret.

The following children were baptized in "Agoste" (Augusta) County
at the "Pinquit Moundyn" (Peaked Mountain), towards the South
"Chanithor" (Shenandoah), in this church at the Mill Creek, or in
their homes:
Anna Catharine Lang (Long) of Henry and Anna Catharine, nee
Wentz, bapt. April 25, (1762). Spon: Anna Catharine Wentz,
widow of Valentine Wentz.
John Christian Biedefisch (Peterfish) of Conrad and Catharine, nee
Roth, bapt. July 2. Spon: Parents.
Catharine Eberhardt of Christian and Maria Sophia, nee Carl, bapt.
July 2. Spon: Widow Catharine Wentz.
Anna Maria Hammer of Jacob and Fredericka Rosina, nee
Leuthmanns Leonhard, bapt. July 2. Spon: Gottfried Christian
Leuthmanns Leonhardt, the Lutheran schoolmaster and wife
Anna Maria.
John William Hetterich (Hedrick) of John, Reformed elder, and

Susanna, nee Hornung, bapt. August 29. Spon: Carl Risch (Rush), Lutheran elder, and wife Maria Elisabeth.

Barbara Zimmermann of George, Reformed elder, and Anna, nee Schulteli, bapt. August 29. Spon: Parents.

Anna Maria Mueller of Jacob and Maria Barbara, nee Chrombohr, bapt. August 29. Spon: Charles Mann and wife Anna Maria.

Esther Stoll (Stull) of Frederick and Charlotte, nee Ritter, bapt. August 29. Spon: Parents.

Henry William Manger (Munger) of William and Susanna, nee Brodbeck, bapt. December 5. Spon: Nicholas Mildenberger and wife Barbara.

1763, the following children were baptized in this church at the "Pinquit Moundyn," in Virginia, on Wednesday, August 3, after the sermon:

John Peter Risch of Charles and Maria Elisabeth, nee Suess. Spon: Peter Mueller and wife Maria Margaret.

Anna Maria Bentz (Pence) of Jacob and Catherine, nee Perschinger. Spon: Anna Maria Nicolaus, single.

Jacob Mueller (Miller) of Peter and Margaret, b. April 17, 1765; bapt. June 18. Spon: Jacob Cropp and wife Barbara.

Augustin Ermentraut of Frederick and Catharine, b. January 22, 1765; bapt. May 18. Spon: Augustin Preisch and wife Elisabeth.

John Henry Ermentraut of Frederick and Catharine, b. May 8; bapt. June 19, 1763. Spon: Charles Hetterich, single.

Jacob Argebrecht of Jacob and Susanna, b. August 26, 1762; bapt. February 14, 1763. Spon: Jacob Nicolaus and wife Barbara.

John George Argebrecht of Jacob and Susanna, b. January 13, 1765; bapt. Jan. 18. Spon: George Mallo and wife Barbara.

John Charles Manger of William and Susanna, b. November --, 1764; bapt. February 10, 1765. Spon: Charles Roesch and wife Elisabeth.

--- and --- Ermentraut of Henry and Magdalene, b. September 1, 1769; bapt. October 7, 1769. Spon: Frederick Ermentraut and wife Catharine and Elisabeth Ermentraut.

Jacob Metzger of Valentine and Mary Elisabeth, b. April 16, 1764; bapt. May 20. Spon: Jacob Argebrecht and wife Susanna.

Elisabeth Witmann of ---, b. ---, bapt. ---. Spon: Caspar Vogt and wife Elizabeth.

John Jacob Hederich of Charles and Barbara, b. April 11, 1765;

bapt. June 18. Spon: Jacob Conrad.

Magdalene Mann of George Adam and Maria Elisabeth, b. March 11, 1765; bapt. June 18. Spon: Philip Willems and Gertrude Schell, both single.

John Cropp of Jacob and Anna Barbara, b. March 9, 1765; bapt. June 18. Spon: John Argebrecht and Catharine Vogt.

1763, the following children were baptized in the province of Virginia, at the "Pinquit Moundyn," in the church near Mr.Hermann's mill:

Anna Elisabeth Deiss (Dice) of Matthew and Eva Catharine, nee Herrber, bapt. August 28, 1763. Spon: Philip Herrber (Harper), senior elder of the Upper tract, and wife Anna Elisabeth.

Anna Maria Christina Herrloss of Martin and Catharine, nee Lingel, bapt. Oct. 10. Spon: Christopher Kisseling (Kising) and wife Christina.

Anna Barbara Mueller of Peter and Maria Margaret, nee Pick, b. September 23; bapt. December 5. Spon: Jacob Nicolaus and wife Barbara.

George Mann of George and Elisabeth, nee Hermann, b. October 9; bapt. December 5. Spon: Jacob Mann and wife Barbara.

John Caspar Vogt of John Caspar and Elisabeth, nee Wilkiss, bapt. December 5. Spon: Jacob Arkebrecht, Peter Mueller and Catharine Margaret Vogt.

Mary Margaret Ermentraudt of George and Barbara, nee Friedtel (Friddle), bapt. December 5. Spon: Anna Elisabeth Ermentraudt, her grandmother.

Anna Maria Bentz of Jacob and Catharine, b. February 28, 1763; bapt. August 29. Spon: Jacob Nicolaus and wife Barbara and daughter Anna Maria.

George Bentz of Jacob and Catharine, b. August 18, 1764; bapt. October 15. Spon: George Bentz and Sarah Bentz.

Catharine Barbara of Jacob and Elisabeth, b. December 28, 1764; bapt February 10, 1765. Spon: John Votsch and wife Catharine.

Anna Elisabeth Mallo of George and Anna Barbara, b. Jan. 12, 1765; bapt. February 10. Spon: Charles Roesch (Rush) and wife Elisabeth.

Michael Mallo of George and Anna Barbara, b. January 29, 1757. Spon: Michael Mallo and Barbara Ebermann.

Catharine Mallo of George and Anna Barbara, b. August 12, 1758. Spon: George Foltz (Fultz) and wife Catharine.

Anna Maria Mallo of George and Anna Barbara, b. February 19,
1763. Spon: Daniel Krob and Anna Mary Ergenbrecht.
John Mallo of George and Anna Barbara, b. 1768; bapt. on the 23d
of the month. Spon: John Risch and Catharine Miller.
John Adam Hermann (Harman) of Jacob and Anna Christina, b.
March 4, 1755. Spon: George Mann and Anna Maria Hermann.
Anna Maria Hermann (Harman) of Jacob and Anna Christina, b.
May 3, 1757. Spon: George Adam Mann and Anna Maria
Hermann.
Henry Hermann (Harman) of Jacob and Anna Christina, b. August
4, 1759. Spon: Theobald Hermann and wife Sarah.
Elisabeth Hermann (Harman) of Jacob and Anna Christina, b.
October 4, 1761. Spon: Augustin Breiss (Price) and wife
Elisabeth.
Anna Catharine Hermann (Harman) of Jacob and Anna Christina,
b. March 1763. Spon: Anna Catharine Hermann.
Jacob Hermann (Harman) of Jacob and Anna Christina, b. March 9,
1766. Spon: George Mallo and wife Barbara.

On October 23, 1768, the Lutheran and Reformed Union church at
the "Bicket Maundy," in Augusta County, was dedicated by the
Rev. Mr. Schwarbach, Evangelical Lutheran pastor at the
present time.
Daughter Stoll (Stull) of Frederick and wife, bapt. February 14,
1770. Spon: John Clemens and Christina Pesor.
John Mann of George Adam and Elisabeth, bapt. July 20, 1771.
Spon: John Mann and wife Susanna.

On October 8, 1776, Rev. Jacob Frank baptized:
Ann Catharine Magert of David and Susanna, b. April 16. Spon:
Paul Lingel and Anna Catherine.
John George Hartman of John and Christina, b. August 1. Spon:
Paul Lingel and Anna Catherine.

On October 9, 1776:
Mary Catharine Grub of Daniel and Elisabeth, b. December 15,
1775. Spon: Peter Miller and wife Anna Maria.
John Philip Schaeffer (Shaver) of George and Maria Elisabeth, b.
December 29, 1775. Spon: Charles Risch and Maria Elisabeth.
Adam Moll of Henry and Margaret, b. December 22, 1775. Spon:
Adam Herman and Catharine Malvina.

Barbara Finder of Martin and Barbara, b. February 24,1776. Spon:
Jacob Grub and Barbara.
Sarah Preiss of Daniel and Catharine, b. August 20, 1776. Spon:
Matthias Schuler (Shuler) and Elisabeth.
John Lingel of Phillip and Barbara, b. February 10, 1776. Spon:
John Hartman and Christina.
John Manger (Munger) of John and Anna, b. June 2, 1776. Spon:
John Heller and Elisabeth.
Philip Conrad of George and Catharine, b. March 8, 1776. Spon:
Peter Brummer and Catharine.
Anna Maria Heller of John and Elisabeth, b. September 7, 1776.
Spon: John Adam Heller and Barbara.
Jacob Ermentraut of Peter and Catharine, b. August 12, 1776.
Spon: Jacob Argebrecht (Argenbright) and Susanna.
Catherine Ermentraut of Philip and Eva, b.August 23, 1776. Spon:
Frederick Ermentraut and Catharine.
Elisabeth Heller of Adam and Anna Barbara, b. March 15, 1776.
Spon: John Heller and Elizabeth.
Catherine Schramm of Theobald and Anna, b. March 5, 1776. Spon:
Michael Traut (Trout) and Catherine Kohler.
Jonathan Lehmann of George and Elisabeth, b. March 2, 1776.
Spon: Leonard Miller and Catharine.
Adam Geiger of Christian and Margaret, b. July 30, 1776. Spon:
Adam Argebrecht and Elisabeth.
John Michael Reinhardt of Lewis (Ludwig) and Elisabeth, b.
September 18, 1776. Spon: Charles Fey and Dorothy.
John Koehler (Kaylor) of Michael and Elisabeth, b. February 2,
1776. Spon: John Beyer and Eva.

Baptisms entered by Rev. Jacob Frank:
Anna Maria Ermentraut of John and Catherine, b. April 6, 1776.
Spon: Peter Miller and Anna Maria.
Christian Nadler of Sebastian and Sophia, b. January 20, 1776.
Spon: Conrad Bietefisch (Peterfish) and Catherine.
Anna Maria Miller of Peter and Elisabeth, b. February 20, 1776.
Spon: Anthony Oehler and Catherine.
Adam Noll (Null) of Henrich and Margaret, b. ---.
Catherine Risch of John and Anna Maria, b. July 17, 1776. Spon:
Catherine Winkhaus and Michael Traudt.
John Philip Koeller of Lewis and Gertrude, b. April 8, 1776. Spon:

John Tanner and Catherine.
Catherine Tanner of John and Catherine, b. ---. Spon: Catherine
 Miller.
Margaret Runckel of Peter and Margaret, b. April 4, 1776. Spon:
 Mathias Kersch and Margaret.
David Fotsch of Conrad and Maria Magdalene, b. June 25, 1776.
 Spon: David Fotsch (Fox).
Jacob Demuth of Henry and Margaret, b. ---. Spon: Jacob Julius
 and ---.
Elisabeth Preisch of August and Mary, b. July 27, 1776. Spon:
 Augustin Preisch and Elisabeth.

Barbara Beyer of John and Eva, b. March 17, 1775; bapt. April 18,
 1775. Spon: Grandparents.

Anthony Oehler (Eiler) m. Anna Catherine Elisa Smith in the year
 1753, on September 4. Their children were:
Anna Margaret, b. June 12, 1755. Spon: Michael Bitner and Anna
 Margaret.
John, b. March 30, 1757. Spon: John Bretzs and Elisa Schmit.
Anna Barbara, b. November 15, 1759. Spon: Anna Barbara Smith.
Anna Catherine, b. January 25, 1762. Spon: Philip Fischborn
 (Fishburn) and Anna Catherine.
John George, b. June 30, 1764. Spon: John George Schmit and
 Anna Margaret Ament.
Anna Susanna, b. February 11, 1766. Spon: Philip Armbrister and
 Christina.
Anna Maria, b. September 20, 1769. Spon: John Peter Mueller and
 Anna Maria.
Magdalene, b. September 21, 1772; bapt. Oct. 25. Spon: Magdalene
 Ermentraut.

On June 16, 1783, the following children were baptized in the
 "Pickit Mountain" church by Rev. Mr. Schmidt:
Elisabeth Pence of Adam and Margaret, b. April 23. Spon:
 Elisabeth Ergebrecht.
Mary Magdalene Roo (Ruh) of Abraham and Margaret, b. April 3.
 Spon: Anna Maria Zeller (Sellers).
Mary Elisabeth Schneider of Martin and Mary, b. April 25. Spon:
 Jacob Lingel and Catherine.

Mary Margaret Hini (Heine) of William and Margaret, b. December 24, 1778. Spon: Martin Schneider (Snyder) and Mary.

Mary Margaret Boyer (Beyer) of John and Eva, b. June 1, 1781; bapt. July 13, 1781. Spon: Matthias Kirsch and Anna Margaret.

Salome Zimmermann of George, Sr. and Anna, b. August 22,1771; bapt.July 13, 1783.

William Zimmerman of George, Sr. and Anna, b. May 28, 1775; bapt. July 13, 1783.

Henry Zimmerman of George, Sr. and Anna, b. May 12, 1778; bapt. July 13, 1783.

Sarah Risch of John and Anna Maria, b. March 10; bapt. June 16, 1783. Spon: Peter Nicolas, Jr.

Baptized June 16, 1783, by Rev. Mr. Schmidt:

Barbara Prisch of Augustin and Margaret, b. December 7, 1782. Spon: Barbara Miller.

Anna Maria Prisch of Frederick and Catherine, b. February 8. Spon: Anna Maria Prisch and Michael Mallo.

Frederick Ronckel of Lewis and Catherine, b. February 15. Spon: Frederick Hene and wife.

Michael Brisch of Conrad and Elisabeth, b. February 16. Spon: Michael Mallo.

George Becker (Baker) of Lewis and Anna Maria, b. February 8. Spon: George Ergebrecht and Elisabeth Herman.

George Weber of George and Catherine, b. October 23, 1782. Spon: Parents.

Elisabeth Berry of Garret and Mary, b. April 13. Spon: Augustin Prisch, Jr., and wife.

Christina Kissling of Jacob and Barbara, b. June 5. Spon: Christine Baer (Bear).

Catherine Stein of Peter and Elisabeth, b. April 22. Spon: Charles Schmidt and Catherine Ermentraut.

On April 25, 1784, the following children were baptized in this church by Rev. Mr. Schmidt:

Zachariah Schmidt of Charles and Anna Maria, b. February 24, 1784. Spon: Frederick Miller and Elisabeth Herman.

Margaret Prisch of Augustin, Jr. and Margaret, b. March 16. Spon: John Risch and Anna Maria.

John Peter Mallo of George, Jr. and Catherine, b. January 30.

Spon: Peter Prisch and Elisabeth Mallo.
Anna Margaret Venus of Henry and Margaret, b. February 23.
Spon: Jacob Herman and wife.
Anna Margaret Bright (Brett) of John and Catherine, b. January 26.
Spon: Augustin Prisch, Jr. and wife.
John Geyger of Christian and Margaret, b. April 10. Spon: Jacob
Ergebright, Jr. and Elisabeth Ermentraut.
Elisabeth Hamann of Jacob and Elisabeth, b. October 7, 1783.
Spon: Widow Reiss.
Barbara Pence of Henry and Susanna, b. September 22, 1783. Spon:
Adam Pens and Margaret.

On June 6, 1784, the following children were baptized by Rev. Mr.
Schmidt:
Catherine Barki (Birke) of John and Sarah, b. May 4. Spon: Her
grandmother Catherine Pens.
Anna Barbara Pens of George and Margaret, b. July 29, 1783. Spon:
Parents.
David Mann of George Adam and Elisabeth, b. March 10. Spon:
John Beyer and Eva.

On June 27, 1784, the following children were baptized by Rev. Mr.
Schmidt:
William Mildeberger of John and Anna, b. May 25, 1784. Spon:
Parents.
Jacob Koch (Cook) of Henry and Magdalene, b. May 25, 1784. Spon:
William Trarbach (Trobaugh) and wife.
Mary Juliana Risch of George and Mary, b. September 1, 1784; bapt.
November 2. Spon: Grandmother.
Catherine Schneider of Martin and Mary, b. October 5, 1784; bapt.
November 2. Spon: Parents.

On April 20, 1785, the following children were baptized in this
church by Rev. Mr. Schmidt:
Anna Barbara Niclas of Peter and Anna Marg. Elisabeth, b. Feb. 12.
Spon: Her grandmother, Anna Barbara Niclas.
Augustin Prisch of Conrad and Elisabeth, b. March 5, 1785. Spon:
Augustin Prisch and Anna Margaret.
Sarah Prisch (Preus) of Frederick and Anna Catherine, b. March 31,
1785. Spon: George Mallo and Anna Catherine.

Anna Maria Miller of Peter and Anna Barbara, b. June 13, 1785.
Spon: Grandmother.

On September 11, 1785, the following children were baptized by
Rev. Gottlieb Abraham Deschler:
John Frederick Michel of William and Elisabeth, b. August 27, 1785.
Spon: John Frederick Michel (Michael) and Elisabeth.
Elisabeth Frazor of James and Elisabeth, b. June 19, 1785. Spon:
Margaret Hoffman.
John George Boyer of John and Eva, b. July 18. Spon: John George
Koehler and Mary Elisabeth Mallo.

On October 25, 1785, was baptized by Rev. Abraham G. Deschler:
Jacob Ruh of Abraham and Margaret, b. August 10. Spon: John
Winberg and Anna Maria.

On December 25, 1785, was baptized by Rev. Abr. G. Deschler:
John Jacob Schmidt of Charles and Anna Maria, b. November 14,
1785. Spon: John Jacob Ergebrecht, Jr. and Anna Catherine
Hermann.

On August 20, 1786, were baptized by the Reformed minister,
Frederick Henry Giese:
John Mallo of George and Catherine, b. June 4, 1786. Spon: John
Pentz and Marie Catherine Preiss.
John Miller of Peter and Anna Barbara, b. August 2. Spon: John
Risch and Anna Maria.
Barbara Kugler of George and Elisabeth, b. June 4, 1786. Spon:
Jacob Kissling (Kisling) and Anna Barbara.
John Henry Kissling of Jacob and Barbara, b. January 3. Spon:
Jacob Baer, Jr.

On September 10, 1786, were baptized by Rev. Mr. Ronckel:
Anna Barbara Mallo of Michael and Christina, b. August 25, 1786.
Spon: Grandparents.
Anna Maria Prisch of Augustin and Margaret, b. July 5. Spon:
Anna Maria Prisch.

On November 19, 1786, was baptized by Rev. John Jacob Weymar:
Elisabeth Prisch of Conrad and Elisabeth, b. September 11, 1786.

Spon: Peter Preisch and Elisabeth Hermann.

On May 4, 1788, were baptized by Rev. Christian Streit:
Anna Maria Schmidt of Charles and Anna Maria, b. September 13,
   1787. Spon: John Risch (Rush) and Anna Maria.
Elisabeth Miller of Henry and Anna Maria, b. February 22, 1788.
   Spon: Grandmother Miller.
Jacob Nicholas of Peter and Juliana, b. September 9, 1787. Spon:
   Jacob Nicholas.
Elisabeth Miller of Peter and Barbara, b. January 30, 1788. Spon:
   Elisabeth Nicholas.
Anna Barbara Nicholas of Henry and Magdalene, b. February 27,
   1788. Spon: Grandmother Nicholas.
Christian Kaul of William and Anna Barbara, b. December 22, 1787.
   Spon: Parents.
Anna Catherine Hau of Christopher and Elisabeth, b. October 10,
   1787. Spon: George Mallo, Jr. and Anna Catherine.
George Pens of Adam and Margaret, b. January 16, 1788. Spon:
   George Pens, Jr., single.
Juliana Prisch of Augustin and Margaret, b. December 15, 1787.
   Spon: Peter Nicholas and Juliana.

Baptized on October 19, 1788, by Rev. Jacob Weymar:
Anna Maria Nicholas of Peter and Juliana, b. October 9, 1788.
   Spon: John Risch and Anna Maria.

Baptized on June 7, 1789, by Rev. Jacob Weymar:
Sarah Jackson of Wm. and Margaret, b. July 19, 1787. Spon:
   Christian Geiger and Margaret.
George Charles Jackson of Wm. and Margaret, b. December 28,
   1788. Spon: Charles Schmidt and Anna Maria.
Frederick Prisch of Conrad and Elisabeth, b. July 27, 1788. Spon:
   Frederick Prisch and Catherine.
Elisabeth Mallo of George and Anna Catherine, b. December 30,
   1788. Spon: Augustin Prisch and wife.
Maria Barbara Schneider of Martin and Anna Maria, b. October 19,
   1788. Spon: George Kirsch and Margaret Lingel.
Anna Maria Kissling of Jacob and Barbara, b. September 6, 1788.
   Spon: Martin Schneider and wife.
Anna Maria Geiger of Christian and Margaret, b. March 28, 1789.

Spon: Henry Pens and Susanna.
Jacob Michael of Wm. and Elisabeth, b. May 23, 1789. Spon: Jacob
    Mann.
Elisabeth Hene of Jonas and Christina, b. May 18, 1789. Spon:
    Catherine Hene.

Baptized on November 22, 1789, by Rev. Wm. Carpenter:
George Michael Schmidt of Charles and Anna Maria, b. September
    29, 1789. Spon: George Mallo, Sr. and Anna Barbara.
Barbara Risch of John and Anna Maria, b. November 13, 1789.
    Spon: Peter Miller and Barbara.
Margaret Miller of Peter and wife, b. March 18, 1790; bapt. October
    1, 1791.
Anna Maria Wetzel of Christopher and wife, b. April 25, 1791; bapt.
    July 19.
Daughter Risch of John and wife, b. January 15, 1791; bapt. October
    16, 1791.

This baptismal register was written by me, Peter Ahl, and begun
    March 1, 1792:
George Mallo of George and wife, b. July 31, 1791; bapt. February
    19, 1792. Spon: George Heyne.
John George Hau of Christopher, b. October 1, 1791; bapt. April 8,
    (1792). Spon: John George Ermentraut.
Elisabeth Preiss of Frederick, b. March 9, 1791; bapt. April 8. Spon:
    John Mann and Catherine Koehler.
John Matthias Reiner of Francis, b. January 31, 1792; bapt. April 8.
    Spon: Matthias Kirsch.
Elisabeth Menner of Christopher, b. December 19, 1791; bapt. April
    8. Spon: Frederick Preiss.
John George Schillinger of Adam, b. February 27, 1791; bapt. April
    8. Spon: John George Mann.
John Peter Geiger of Christian, b. November 22, 1791; bapt. April 8.
    Spon: Jacob Argenbrecht.
Michael Preiss of Peter, b. May 11, 1792; bapt. June 4. Spon:
    William Michel.
Anna Maria Preiss of Conrad, b. January 5; bapt. June 17, 1792.
    Spon: Peter Preiss (Price) and wife.
Christina Kissling of Henry, b. June 7, 1791; bapt. June 18, 1792.
    Spon: Christian Hartmann.

Catherine Ahl of Peter, b. June 5; bapt. June 14, 1792. Spon:
George Mallo and Catherine.

John George Wagner of George, b. June 14, 1792; bapt. July 22.
Spon: George Mallo and wife.

Henry Preiss (Price) of Peter, b. November 29, 1790; bapt. Dec. 12.
Spon: Henry Mueller and wife.

Mary Catherine Ermentraut (Armentrout) of John, b. July 4; bapt.
August 4. Spon: Catherine Ermentraut.

Sarah Miller of Henry, b. 1791; bapt. September 21. Spon: George
Mallo.

Anna Kissling of Jacob, b. 1792; bapt. February 26. Spon: Jacob
Miller.

Catherine Hellendahl (Helmenthal) of Jacob, b. 1792; bapt. July 20.
Spon: Catherine Herman.

John Henry Luecke of Christian, b. May 26, 1792; bapt. December 2.
Spon: William Hettrich.

Anna Elisabeth Ruesch of John, b. October 11, 1792; bapt. January
26, 1793. Spon: Anna Elisabeth Niclas.

John Matthias Schneyder (Snyder) of Martin, b. January 4; bapt.
Jan. 26, 1793. Spon: Matthias Kirsch.

Catherine Mueller of Peter, b. December 26, 1792; bapt. February
24, (1793). Spon: John Ermentraut and wife.

John George Ermentraut of Augustin, b. April 26, 1793; bapt. May
12, (1793). Spon: John George Ermentraut.

Abraham Fey of John and Susanna, b. October 29, 1792; bapt. June
23, 1973. Spon: Parents.

Eva Neu of Peter and Juliana, b. October 30, 1792; bapt. June 23,
1793. Spon: Maria Kissling.

Sarah Hardman of John and Anna Maria, b. June 2, 1793; bapt.
June 23, 1793. Spon: Peter Neu and Juliana.

John Jacob Hoehn of Jonas, b. July 1, 1793; bapt. July 22, 1793.
Spon: John Jacob Kirsch.

John Beyer of John, b. May 2; bapt. August 18, 1793. Spon: Martin
Schneider and wife.

John George Preuss of Frederick, b. December 13, 1792; bapt.
February 3, 1794. Spon: George Mallo.

John Peter Preuss of Conrad, b. December 5, 1792; bapt. February
3, 1794. Spon: Peter Preuss.

Eva Catherine Reinert of Francis, b. September 20, 1793; bapt.
March 2, 1794. Spon: Eva Catherine Hauel.

Peter Preuss of Peter, b. April 2, 1794; bapt. June 24, 1794. Spon:
Frederick Preuss.
John Wagner of George, b. February 28, 1794; bapt. June 29, 1794.
Spon: Peter Preuss.
Christina Preuss of Augustin, b. July 2, 1793; bapt. July 20, 1794.
Spon: John Weyberg.
Anna Elisabeth Geiger of Frederick, b. December 1, 1794; bapt.
February 10, 1795. Spon: Christian Lucke and wife Elisabeth.
John Reyer of Philip, b. December 8, 1794; bapt. February 19, 1795.
Spon: John Reyer (Royer) and wife Elisabeth.
John Ruesch of John, b. November 30, 1794; bapt. March 8, 1795.
Spon: John Reyer (Royer) and wife Elisabeth.
John Peter Miller of Peter, b. August 3, 1794; bapt. August 12, 1794.
Spon: Peter Nicholas and wife.

On March 6, 1796, the following children were baptized in this
church at the Peaked Mountain by Rev. V. G. C. Stochus:
Elizabeth Wagner of George, b. October 22, 1795. Spon: Martin
Schneider and wife.
Isaac Hatfield of Edward, b. October 28, 1795. Spon: Martin
Schneider and wife.
Sally Reinert of Francis, b. September 8, 1795. Spon: George
Mallow.
Christian Ermentraut of Frederick, b. January 1, 1796. Spon:
Frederick Geiger.

On the last of March, 1796:
Anne Elisabeth Miller of Peter, b. February 8, 1796. Spon: Anna
Elisabeth ⋯.
Anna Maria Koenig of Henry, b. February 15. Spon: Anna Maria
Argebrecht.
Elisabeth Lichy (Luecke) of Christian, b. February 23. Spon: Peter
Nicolaus.
Mary Elisabeth Spilky of Gottfried, b. December 28, 1795.
Christopher Werbel (Wirbel) of Christopher, b. February 28; bapt.
March 27. Spon: Christopher Ermentraut and wife.
Jacob Heyl of Jacob, b. April 3; bapt. April 17, (1796). Spon:
Christopher Werbel and wife.
Barbara Heyl of Jacob, b. March 8, 1795; bapt. April 17, (1796).
Spon: Catherine Sprenckelsen.

Margaret Zeller (Sellers) of John, b. February 12, 1796; bapt. April 17, (1796). Spon: Margaret Manger.

Joseph Smith of James, b. March 12, 1795; bapt. April 17, 1796. Spon: David Manger.

Elisabeth Kissling of Jacob, b. March 4, 1796; bapt. April 17, 1796. Spon: Margaret Ermentraut.

Juliana Wetzel of Christopher, b. March 30, 1795; bapt. May 5, 1796. Spon: Peter Nicholas.

Elisabeth Andre of Adam, b. April 19, 1795; bapt. May 8, 1796. Spon: Parents.

Hannah Oche of John, b. January 6, 1795; bapt. May 8, 1796. Spon: John Megert.

Anna Maria Nunnemacher of Daniel, b. June 27, 1796; bapt. July 26. Spon: Philip Reyer.

Mary Elisabeth Bertram of Julius, b. June 14, 1794; bapt. February 11, 1796. Spon: Martin Schneider.

John Bertram of Julius, b. July 22, 1796; bapt. August 21. Spon: John Bentz.

Abraham Oche of John, b. July 11, 1796; bapt. August 21. Spon: Henry Manger.

John George Koehler of John George, b. July 27; bapt. September 18, (1796). Spon: John Jacob Risch.

Anna Maria Risch of Peter, b. October 2; bapt. October 10 (died on same day). Spon: Charles Risch and wife, her grandparents.

Henry Algebrecht of Jacob, b. October 31, 1796; bapt. March 12, 1797. Spon: Henry Bentz.

Mary Catherine Ermentraut of Christopher, b. November 12, 1796; bapt. March 12, 1797. Spon: Mary Catherine Ermentraut.

John Schaefer of Jacob, b. February 8, 1797; bapt. April 2, 1797. Spon: Parents.

Eva Elisabeth Hain of Jonas, b. April 12; bapt. May 2, 1797. Spon: John Beyer and wife.

John Frederick Kirchhoff of Christopher, b. November 29, 1796; bapt. May 14, 1797. Spon: John Busch (Bush) and Cath. Mallow.

John Zeller of Henry and Magdalene, b. March 11, 1797; bapt. June 24, 1797. Spon: William Hedrich and wife.

John Bens of John, b. May 27; bapt. July 30, (1797). Spon: Henry Bens (Pence).

Elisabeth Ryer (Royer) of Philip, b. July 2; bapt. July 30, (1797). Spon: Peter Ryer.

Anna Maria Mallo of George, b. July 26; bapt. August 6, (1797).
Spon: Martin Schneider.

Peter Nunnemacher of Daniel, b. August 2; bapt. September 3,
(1797). Spon: (?)Elis. Koehler.

Jacob Miller of Peter and Barbara, b. September 28, 1797; bapt.
October 2, 1797. Spon: Jacob Nicklas and wife.

Elisabeth Reiner(t) of Francis, b. January 24, 1798; bapt. March 11.
Spon: Philip Lung (Long).

Jacob Schaefer of Jacob and Mary, b. January 12; bapt. March 11,
1798. Spon: Parents.

Jacob Wagener (Waggoner) of George, b. December 30, 1797; bapt.
March 11, (1798). Spon: Jacob Nicklaus.

John Reb of Jacob, b. October 8; bapt. March 11, (1798). Spon:
George Mallo.

Anna Margaret Reb of Jacob, b. February 25; bapt. April 8, (1798).
Spon: David Manger.

Jacob Koenig of Henry, b. ---.

John Henry Bertram of Julius, b. February 19, 1798; bapt. April 8,
1798. Spon: John Michael and Cath. Laugs.

John Jacob Henh of John, b. February 15, 1798; bapt. April 8,
(1798). Spon: John Jacob Risch.

Lydia Geiger of Christian, b. August 29, 1798. Spon: Margaret
Bens (Pence).

John Frederick Spilke of Gottfried, b. September 24, 1797; bapt.
November 9, 1797. Spon: George Koeler (Kaylor).

Daughter Brill of Thomas, b. January 11, 1798; bapt. April 29.
Spon: Jacob Nicklas.

William Becker (Baker) of Conrad, b. March 29, 1798; bapt. May 25.

Daughter Faluers of Adam and Maria, b. April 5, 1798; bapt.
November 11, 1798. Spon: Eva Schuh.

Daughter Reusch of Peter and Barbara, b. May 29, 1798; bapt.
November 11, 1798. Spon: Charles Reusch and wife Mary
Elizabeth.

Daughter Koehler of George and Catherine, b. April 18, 1798; bapt. -
--. Spon: Jacob Reb and wife Catherine.

Valentin Ermentrout of Frederick and Elizabeth, b. September 24;
bapt. November 10, 1799. Spon: Augustin Ermentrout and wife
Margaret.

John George Bertram of Julius and Eva, b. October 28; bapt.
November 10, 1799. Spon: George Melle and wife Catherine.

Jacob Nunnemacher of Daniel and Mary, b. May 17, 1799. Spon:
Jacob Argebrecht.

Annie Maria Reur (Royers) of Peter and Elizabeth, b. February 26,
1799. Spon: Catherine Reyer.

Philip Rey(er) of Philip and Catherine, b. July 6, 1799. Spon: John
Koeler.

John Ayler (Eiler) of Peter and Elizabeth, b. November 10, 1798.
Spon: John Resch.

Daughter Nicklaus of Jacob and Elizabeth, b. May 28, 1798. Spon:
Mary Risch.

Mary Nicklaus of Jacob and Elizabeth, b. September 8, 1799; bapt.
November 10, 1799. Spon: Mary Risch.

Polly Reinert of Francis, b. December 31, 1799; bapt. June 2, 1800.
Spon: Elizabeth Schneider.

Anna Eichelbrecht (Elizabeth) of Jacob and Mary, b. December 10,
1799; bapt. June 2, 1800. Spon: Peter Mueller and Barbara.

John Penns of Henry and Catherine, b. December 13, 1799; bapt.
June 2, 1800. Spon: John Penns.

Anna Zeller of Peter and Magdalene, b. November 2, 1799; bapt.
June 2, 1800. Spon: Thomas Brill and Anna Maria.

Anna Maria Zeller of John and Eva, b. January 1, 1800; bapt. June
2, 1800. Spon: Anna Maria Zeller.

Henry Miller of Peter and Barbara, b. January 18, 1800; bapt. June
2, 1800. Spon: Jacob Ergebrecht and wife Mary.

Elizabeth Koehler of George and Catherine, b. --- 21, 1790; bapt.
June 2, 1800. Spon: Philip Reyer and Catherine.

Catherine Geiger of Fr. and Barbara, b. February 17, 1800; bapt.
June 2. Spon: Christian Geiger and Catherine.

Anna Mallo of George and Catherine, b. March 26, 1800; bapt. June
2, 1800. Spon: Jacob Kissling and Barbara.

George Nicklas of Jacob and Elizabeth, b. April 3,1801. Spon: John
Nicklas.

Immanuel Ermentraut of August and Margaret, b. June 15, 1801;
bapt. August 9. Spon: Christian Leuke and Elizabeth.

Samuel Bertram of Julius and Eva, b. 1801; bapt August 9. Spon:
Parents.

William Samrbier of Anthony and Catherine, b. May 9, 1801; bapt
September 6. Spon: George Panther (Painter) and wife Sophia.

William Zehriass of John and Elizabeth, b. June 1801; bapt. Sept 6.
Spon: William Hederich and wife Catherine.

Catherine Hehn of John and Dorothy, b. August 4, 1801; bapt.
    September 6. Spon: Fred.Hehn and wife Catherine.
Oliver Eiler of Peter and Elizabeth, b. July 9, 1801; bapt. August 16.
    Spon: Peter Eyler and Catherine.
Matthew Ermentraut of Fred and Barbara, b. September 8, 1801;
    bapt. November 1, 1801. Spon: George Ermentraut.
Sarah Christ of Henry and Catherine, b. June 27, 1801; bapt.
    November 1, 1801. Spon: Peter Seich and Margaret.
John Frederick Koehler of John and Barbara, b. October 27, 1801;
    bapt. November 1, 1801. Spon: Fred Hehn and Catherine.
Nicholas Miller of Peter and Barbara, b. October 28, 1801; bapt.
    December 27, 1801. Spon: Parents.
John Becker of Christian, b. February 22; bapt. April 16, 1802.
    Spon: Thomas Brill and wife.
John Keller of George, b. January 26; bapt. April 16, 1802. Spon:
    John Keller and wife.
Anna Catherine Geret (Garriott) of Samuel and Sarah, b. April 13,
    1802; bapt. June 13, 1802. Spon: George Mueller and wife
    Catherine.
John Christopher Wetzel of Christopher and Ursula, b. May 19,
    1802; bapt. June 13, 1802. Spon: John Beyer and wife Eva.
John Hoerner of Henry and Elizabeth, b. March 13, 1802; bapt. June
    13, 1802. Spon: Henry Penns.

Marriages in 1762:
Jacob Kropp (Cropp), son of Christian Kropp and Anna Barbara
    Metzger, dau. of George Valentine Metzger, m. March 2.
Peter Mueller, son of Henry Mueller, and Margaret Kropp, dau. of
    Christian Kropp, m. March 2.
George Schillinger, widower and Anna Elizabeth Horning, widow of
    Mr. Conrad Stehlmann, m. October 4, 1762.
George Adam Mann, single and Elizabeth Hermann, single, m.
    December 7, 1762.

Confirmations:
On Saturday, February 27, 1762, Margaret Kropp (Cropp).
On Saturday, April 24, 1762, were confirmed and on Sunday, April
    25 admitted to the Lord's Supper:
John Henry Ermentraudt (Armentrout)
Catherine Gall, wife of Jacob Guthmann, and Anna Barbara Diether

(Dietrick).

Deaths, burials in grave yard of church:
Elizabeth Schaefer (Shaver), b. November 21, 1727; d. November 6,
    1795; bur. on the 8th inst., aged 17 yrs. 11 mos. 16 days.
Susanna Schaefer, b. September 30, 1770; d. November 12, 1795;
    bur. on the 14th inst., aged 25 yrs 1 mo. 11 days.
Sarah Schaefer, b. July 12, 1782; d. November 23, 1795; bur. on the
    25th inst., aged 13 yrs. 4 mos. 11 days.
John Michael Schaefer, b. February 6, 1774; d. November 25, 1795;
    bur. on the (27th), aged 21 yrs. 9 mos. 18 days.
William Geiger, b. June 30, 1776; d. December 20, (1795); bur.
    December 22, aged 19 yrs. 6 mos. 20 days.
Elizabeth Ementraut (Amentraut), b. in 1725; d. October 7, 1795;
    bur. on the 8th inst., aged 70 yrs.
Conrad Schneider, b. December 10, 1715; d. October 7; bur. October
    9th, aged 79 yrs. 10 mos. 3 days.
Anna Maria Risch, b. eight days ago; d. February 2, 1796.
George Wagner, b. 1792, d. December 7, 1796; bur. December 8th.
Barbara Mallo, b. September 26, 1726; d. January 17, 1797; bur. on
    the 19th, aged 70 yrs. 3 mos. 22 days.

Marriages at Peaked Mountain, from November 15, 1795-November
    15, 1796, D. C. Stock, minister:
Jacob Schaefer and the daughter of Peter Bietefisch (Peterfish) m.
    June 27.
Christian Geiger, Sr., widower, and widow Dindore (Dundore) m.
    September 6.
George Schaefer and Elizabeth Vogt, daughter of Martin Vogt, elder
    at Peter Ermentraut's church, m. September 30.
Christian Geiger and Emilia Schmidt m. September 25.

FRIEDENS CHURCH

Translated by Rodger Bundy

Baptism and Church Book of the Combined United Congregation at the Frieden Church in Rockingham County Confirmation, Evening Mass and Burial Index Begun from the year after Christ 1786 and this new church book is completed in the year 1795.

Current Directors.

Reformed column	Lutheran column
Leonhard Duttweiler	Leonhard Muller
Johannes Weiss	Johannes Tanner
Peter Braun	Heinrich Deb
Johannes Kiblinger	Ludwig Keller
Johan Beber	Heinrich Kessler
Ulrich Seeler	Adam Pott
Conrad Holire	Jacub Scheuerlye
Abraham Bose	Johannes Weittig
Johannes Kieblinger	Jacob Kesler
Martin Wittmer	Phillipp Keller
Jacob Spaeter Soe..(?)	Johannes Ehrman
Adam Long	Heinrich Schulter
Georg Hollirye	Daniel Schmidt
	Jacob Schmidt

(next page)
Holy Church elders.

Lutheran column	Reformed column
Leonhard Bender	Valentin Hofman
Andreas Huttelloch	Dewald Schram
Jacob Zanger	Peter Braun
Friederich Schwartz	Jacob Schuz
Christoph Schmied	Johann Beber
Leonhard Zimerman	Mathias Willberger
Johannes Chole	Jacob Wittmar
Daniel Duendel	Leonhard Zimerman
Adam Pott	Valentin Saftl(ig?)
Heinrich Kesler	Ulrich Sehler
Heinrich Schulterman	Abraham Bose

Jacob Spaeter, Soe

Currently Active Preachers.

Lutheran column	Reformed column
Gottlieb Teschler	Andreas Loritz
Joh. Georg Bottler	Leonhard Willy
Peter Ahl	Daniel Hoffman
Joseph Windel	Johannes Baunus(?)
Georg Rienien(?)shneider	

----

todays date is 21st Oct 1821 the Colect... had ... and after payment
of all remaining expenses ... and paid to Mr. Martin Wittmar 8
dollars 2 schillings and 3 pence   J.B(rau?)..

Anno 1786
baptised Jul 16th:
to Heironimus Deb and wife Anna Margreth is born Anna
    M(argreth?) 22 Jun 1786 witness Peter Zoller and wife Elisabeth
to Johannes Zehr and wife Elisabeth is born Johanes witness Jacob
    Zehr and wife Chatrina (Huettelloch)
to Valentin Heyser and wife Chatrina is born Eva 26 Jun 1786
    witness Johanes Michael and wife ___
baptised Aug 16th:
to Andreas Wolf and wife Anna Elisabeth is born Maria Elisabeth 25
    Jul 1786 witness Maria Elisabeth godmother
baptised (?) 10th:
to Wilhelm Trorbach and wife Chatrina is born Johan Heinrich 18
    Sep 1785 witness Theobald Schramm and wife Anna
to Johanes Beher and wife Anna is born Susanna 19 Mar 1786
    witness Mathias Willburger and wife Anna Margreth
to Conrad Zoller and wife Madlena is born Anna Christina 7 Apr
    1786 witness Christina Zoller
to Johan Schuz and wife Chatrina is born Chatrina 8 Jul 1786
    witness Georg Schuz and wife Chatrina
to Johanes Langenfulder and wife Madlena is born Johanes 8 Aug
    1785 witness Wilhelm Trorbach and wife Chatrina
baptised (?) 15th:
to Peter Ebersb and wife Margreth is born Christina 19 Jul 1786
    witness Chatrina Huttelloch
baptised (?) 3rd:

to Heinrich Bender and wife Chatrina is born Heinrich 1 Jul 1786
   witness Child's grandfather
to Michael Danner and wife Esther is born Maria Esther 1 Sep 1786
baptised (?) 25th:
to Johanes Wittmar and wife is born ___ 26 Aug 1786 witness
   Valentin Seyler and wife Chatrina

1787
baptised Jan 28th:
to Friedrich Schwartz and wife Anna Maria is born Maria Susanna
   11 Oct 1786 witness Friedrich Schwarz and wife Sabrina
baptised Mar 4th:
to Christian Dutterer and wife Maria Elisabeth is born Johan Jacob
   19 Feb 1787 witness Christian Venus and wife Maria
to Mrs. Magdalena Danner is born Christian 6 Feb 1787 witness
   Leonhard Bender and wife Chatrina
to Ludwig Schreyer and wife Anna Maria is born Salome 15 Aug
   1786 witness Johanes Weiss and wife Chatrina
to Michael Scheyrer and wife Maria Elisabeth is born Maria
   Elisabeth 2 Jun 1787 witness Friedrich Schwarz and wife Salome
baptised (?) 6th:
to Jacob Argobreiht and wife Anna Maria is born Elisabeth 21 Jun
   1786 witness Anna Margreth
to Jacob Argobreiht and wife Elisabeth is born Friedrich 21 Jun
   1786 witness Friedrich Schwarz and wife Salome
to Johanes Dauer and wife Chatrina is born Johan Joseph 20 Aug
   1786 witness Johanes Pott and Anna Maria Pottin
baptised Jul 1st:
to Caspar M..erts and wife Anna Maria is born Anna Maria 6 May
   1786 witness the parents themselves
to Franz Ott and wife Chatrina is born Maria Salome 16 May 1786
   witnesses Friedrich Schwarz and wife Salome
to Christian Pass and wife Susanna is born Elisabeth 9 Jun 1786
to Franz Barth and wife Dorothea is born Elisabeth 10 May 1786
   witness Elisabeth Zangerin
to Eduard Herl and wife Anna is born Eduard .. Oct 1786 witness
   Johanes Kotte and wife Anna Maria
to Wilhelm Wildenberger and wife Chatrina is born Johanes 28 May
   1786 witness Johan Joseph Schwarz and wife Anna

baptised Aug 5th:

to Johanes Dontor(?) and wife Chatrin is born Maria 3 Jun 1786
   witness Maria Delbingerin

baptised (Aug) 13th:

to Jacob Vaz and wife Anna Maria is born Johanes 21 Jul 1786
   witness Valentin Heyser and wife Chatrina

1787

baptised (?) 30th:

to Heinrich Deb and wife Chatrina is born Chatrina Barbara 21 Aug
   1786 witness Leonhard Bender and wife Chatrina

to Peter Weibel and wife Madlena children born (1) Michael in June
   1782 witness Michael Danner and wife Chatrina (2) Heinrich 23
   Oct 1784 witness Heinrich Deb and wife Christina (3) Susanna
   31 May 1787 witness Jacob Bidshong and wife Susanna

1788

baptised (?) 14th:

to Jacob Koch and wife Elisabeth is born Valentin witness Valentin
   Schalle and wife Chatrina

baptised (?) 21st:

to Peter Lahm and wife Chatrina is born Anna Maria 2 Oct 1787
   witness the parents themselves

to Christian Kinzer and wife Chatrina is born Christina 4 Aug 1788

to Paul Schumacher and wife Chatrina is born Andrew 17 Jun 1788
   witness Adam A Binanssel(?) and wife Angina

to Johan Wildenberger and wife Anna is born Johanes

baptised (?) 14th:

to Johanes Weiss and wife Chatrina is born a son David 2 Oct 1787
   witness Adam Weiss

to Heinrich Ernsberger and wife Anna Maria is born Heinrich 2 Jun
   1787

to Adam (?) and wife Barbara is born Johan Adam 24 Oct 1787

baptised (?) 4th:

to Johanes Wilbiner and wife Maria Elisabeth 4 Jul 1788 witness
   Maria Chatrina Traubachin

1789

baptised Apr 10th:

to Michael Kinzer and wife Esther is born Johanes 26 Sep 1788
   witness Jacob Zanger and wife Chatrina

baptised May 14th:
to Garret Talten is born Johanes .. Mar 1789 witness Johanes Pott
    and wife
to Georg Henzel and wife is born Salamon 11 Aug 1789 witness the
    parents themselves
to Mr. Schnepp and wife is born Johanes 21 Sep 1789 witness the
    parents themselves
to Karl Ernsberger and wife is born Heinrich 22 Feb 1789 witness
    the parents themselves
to Henrich Ernsberger and wife is born Jacob 10 Aug 1788 witness
    the parents themselves
to Philipp Kuster and wife is born Johannes 19 Aug 1789 witness
    Johan Klein and wife
baptised Aug 23rd:
to Peter Peb and wife Maria is born Madlena 10 Jun 1789 witness
    Madlena Kiblinger
to Friedrich Kessler and wife Chatrina is born Johanes 23 Aug 1789
    witness David Willberger and wife Christina
to Peter Kothgebb and wife Hanna is born Emanuel 19 Sep 1789
    witness Elisabeth Zoller
1790
baptised April 18th:
to Christian Seeler and wife Margreth is born Barbara 30 Jan 1790
    witness Elisabeth Schleiter
to Peter Braun and wife Elisabeth is born Margreth 20 Feb 1790
    witness Valentin Hofman and wife Maria
to Peter Blecher and wife Elisabeth is born Susann 23 Mar 1790
    witness Heinrich Kessler and wife Barbara

1790
baptised Apr 18th:
to Peter Kuster and wife Elisabeth is born Elisabeth 1 Aug 1789
    witness Johan Klein and wife
to Ludwig Scheyer and wife Anna Maria is born Johan Jacob 6 Jul
    1789 witness Jacob Zanger and wife
to Johan Muller and wife Margreth is born Anna Maria 25 Sep 1789
    witness Peter Zanger and wife Anna Maria
to Franz Ott and wife Chatrina is born Chatrina 1 Feb 1790 witness
    Michael Kinzer and wife Esther
to Johan Kaush(?) and wife Maria Madlena is born Chatrina 22 Mar
    1790 witness Leonhard Muller and wife Chatrina

to Adam Argobreiht and wife Barbara is born Elisabeth 28 Jun 1790
to Jacob Deb and wife Elisabeth is born Jacob 26 Apr 1790 witness
     Valentin Hofman and wife Maria
to Jacob Deb and wife Elisabeth is born Elisabeth 26 Apr 1790
     witness Heinrich Deb and wife Chatrina
baptised Aug 18th:
to Johan Klein and wife Christina is born Daniel 24 Feb 1790
     witness the parents themselves
to Jacob Scheuerman and wife Elisabeth is born Maria 29 Jun 1790
     witness Mrs Maria Lehmann
baptised after Aug ..th:
to Michael Erman and wife Anna Maria is born Joseph Sep 1790
     witness Christian Seeler and wife Margreth
1791
baptised (?) ..th
to Johan Klein and wife Chatrina is born Heinrich 17 Mar 1790
     witness the parents themselves
to Philipp Boehmer and wife Elisabeth is born Sarah 10 Sep 1790
baptised (?) 27th:
to Georg Hoffman and wife Barbara is born Johannes 21 Jan 1791
     witnesses the parents themselves
to Johan Schwarz and wife is born Johan Friederich 2 Feb 1791
     witnesses Valentin Hoffman and wife Maria

1791
baptised (?) 14th:
to David Willberger and wife Chatrina is born Chatrina Appolonia
     May 1791 witness Mrs Elisabeth Zoller
1792
baptised (?) 8th:
to Jacob Scheurer and wife Elisabeth is born Joh. Jacob witness the
     parents themselves
baptised (?) 24th:
to Peter Braun and wife Elisabeth is born Barbara May 1792
     witness Georg Hofman and wife Chatrina
baptised (?) 1st:
to Franz Jacob Ott and wife is born Michael May 1792
to Johanes Weizel and wife is born Johanes
baptised (?) 2nd:
to Michael Nambach and wife Madlena is born Salome Jun 1792

to Philipp Kraft and wife Barbara is born Johanes 16 Apr 1792
witness Franz Johanes Zehrtass and wife ?
baptised (?) 10th:
to Conrad Klein and wife Maria is born Elisabeth 19 Feb 1792
    witness Ulrich Seeler and wife Maria
to Adam Klein and wife Susanna is born Susanna 2 Jul 1792
    witness Eva Schmidt
baptised (?) 12th:
to Friedrich Nambach and wife Margreth is born Salome 18 May
    1792
baptised (?) 9th:
to Peter Kiblinger and wife Salome is born Johanes 16 Jun 1792
    witness Johanes Beber and wife Anna
to Gottlieb Pfeister and wife Dorothea is born Adam 29 Jun 1792
    witness Johanes .eidig and wife Margreth
baptised (?) 23rd:
to Georg Zaug(?) and wife Barbara is born Johan Adam 26 Aug 1792
    witness Jacob Zaug and wife Elisabeth
baptised (?) 7th:
to Samuel Beber and wife Barbara is born Maria Chatrina 22 Aug
    1792 witness Valentin Schalle and wife Anna

1792
baptised (?) 18th:
to Johan Paul and wife Chatrina is born Michael 2 Aug 1792
    witness Michael Kleinfelder
baptised (?) 16th:
to Georg Kleiner and wife Madlena is born Margreth 23 Aug 1792
    witness Gottlieb Pfeifer and wife Dorothea
baptised (?) 25th:
to Daniel Schuz and wife Elisabeth is born Eva Perena(?) 22 Jul
    1792 witness Jacob Schuz and the mother
to Christoph Venus and wife Maria is born Abraham 17 Jul 1792
    witness Jacob Pott and wife Esther
1793
baptised (?) 3rd:
to Georg Hofman and wife Barbara is born Anna Maria 30 Oct 1792
    witness Peter Braun and wife Elisabeth
baptised (?) 24th:
to Wilhelm Trorbach and wife Barbara is born Chatrina Oct 1792

witness Wilhelm Trorbach Sr. and wife
baptised (?) 1st:
to Johan Beber and wife Anna is born Elisabeth Jul 1792 witness
the parents themselves
baptised (?) 19th:
to Michael Kron and wife ? is born Salome Oct 1792
baptised (?) 22nd:
to Maria Wittmar is born an illegitimate child Madlena May 1793
witness Chatrina Willberger
baptised (?) 30th:
to Johan Kiblinger and wife Elisabeth is born Anna 29 Mar 1793
to Johan Pott and wife Maria is born Sarah 2 Aug 1792
to Philipp Kuster and wife Maria is born Sa(lome?) Jun 1793
witness Johan Kuster and Hanna Dutweiler
baptised (?) 25th:
to Heinrich Pott and wife is born Heinrich Jul 1793 witness Adam
Pott and wife
baptised (?) 10th:
to young Duttweiler and wife is born Martin Jul 1793 witness the
parents themselves

1793
baptised (?) 14th:
to Daniel Schuz and wife Chatrina is born Susanna 12 Aug 1793
witness Conrad Holire and wife
baptised (?) 19th:
to Johan Ehrman and wife Chatrina is born Martin Eli Sebastian
Aug 1793 witness Jacob Berby and wife
baptised (?) 21st:
to David Willberger and Barbara Zoller is born an illegitimate child
Migani(?) in May 1793 witness Madlena Zoller
baptised (?) 7th:
to Philipp Hedlig(?) and wife ? is born Philipp 18 Jul 1793 witness
the parents themselves
baptised (?) 8th:
to Adam Schillinger and wife Elisabeth is born Anna Barbara 27
Feb 1793 witness the parents themselves
baptised (?) 12th:
to Wilhelm Gaug(?) and wife Barbara is born Elisabeth 27 Mar
1792(?) witness the parents themselves

to Christian Dutterer and wife Elisabeth is born Maria Chatrina 30
  Jul 1793 witness Maria Schram
to Joseph Lang and wife Elisabeth is born Sarah 12 Feb 1793
  witness Dorothea Tintel
to Ulrich Seeler and wife Maria is born Peter 31 Aug 1793 witness
  Johan Kiblinger and wife Elisabeth
to Johan Krank and wife Elisabeth is born Tainey Aug 1793 witness
  the grandparents of the child
1794
baptised June 26th:
to Philipp Kraft and wife Barbara is born Maria Elisabeth 19 Oct
  1793
to Heinrich Kessler and wife Barbara is born Anna Maria 3 Jun
  1794 witness Migani(?) Teg.....(?) and wife Barbara
to Jacob Pott and wife Esther is born Susanna 14 Jun 1794 witness
  Valentin Hoffman and wife Maria
to Ulrich Seeler and wife Elisabeth is born Anna Margreth 4 Jun
  1794 witness Christian Seeler and wife Anna Margreth

[Page 43]
1794
baptised April 27th:
to Adam Schneider and wife is born Susanna in Feb 1794 witness
  Conrad Holire and wife
baptised May 4th:
to Philipp Boehmer and wife Elisabeth is born Joseph 10 Feb 1794
to Adam Pauler and wife Elisabeth is born Chatrina Elisabeth 20
  Mar 1794 witness Jacob Koch and wife Chatrina Elisabeth
to Adam Haus and wife Chatrina is born Jacob 12 Jun 1794 witness
  Johan Weidig and wife Anna
to Johan Weidig and wife Anna Margreth is born Jeremias 29 Jul
  1793 witness Adam Haus and wife Chatrina
baptised (?) 10th:
to Adam Lang and wife Margreth is born Margreth 13 Apr 1794
  witness Mathias Willberger and wife Maria Margreth
to Johan Graeye and wife Chatrina is born Jonas in Jun 1794
  witness Jacob Schenk and wife Chatrina
to Adam Graeye and wife Elisabeth is born 1. Adam 6 Aug 1792
  witness Chatrina Graeye 2. Chatrina 6 Apr 1794
to Ludwig Keller and wife Sarah is born Jacob witness Adam Pott

to Christian Hofman and wife Barbara is born Valentin witness
Valentin Hofman and wife Maria

to Adam Lingsweiler and wife is born Jacob 18 Feb 1794 witness
    Jacob Kessler and wife

to Conrad Klein and wife is born Susanna 3 Feb 1794 witness Anna
    Maria (Z)auten

to Johanes Fattorf and wife is born Sarah 22 May 1794 witness
    Johanes Weizel and wife

[Page 14]
1794

to Heinrich Schneider and wife is born a daughter - 11 May 1794
    witness Elisabeth Unruh

to Johanes Klein and wife is born a daughter - 17 Jun 1793 witness
    the parents themselves

to Peter Baushlag and wife is born a daughter - 3 Mar 1793 witness
    the parents themselves

to Georg Kehrbach and wife Ziristinge is born Anna and Sarah 26
    Jun 1794 witness Leonhard Dutweiler and wife, Friedrich
    Schwarz and wife

to Johanes Widmore and wife is born a little daughter 24 Jun 1793
    witness Mathias ..an and wife?

to Johanes Bross and wife is born a little daughter 25 Jun 1794 the
    widow Lang

to Heinrich Tauberman and wife is born a little daughter 25 Mar
    1794 witness Jacob Schmid and wife

to Johanes Argobreiht and wife is born Johanes 14 Feb 1794 witness
    Adam Argobreiht and wife

to Peter Zoller and wife is born a little daughter Chatrina 4 Jul 1794
    witness Peter Zoller Sr and wife Elisabeth

to Abraham ficher and wife is born a little son - 5 Aug 1794 witness
    Heinrich Kessler and wife

to Heinrich Zimmerman and wife is born a little son - 4 Aug 1794
    witness Heinrich Berky

to Jacob Schenl and wife is born a little son 3 Jul 1794 witness
    Michael Weiss and wife

to Johanes Weber and wife is born a little daughter - 19 Jul 1794

to Jacob Graeye and wife is born a little daughter - 25 Jul 1794
    witness Peter Koch and wife

[Page 16]
1794
to Jacob Lingenfelder and wife is born Johanes 25 Jul 1794 witness
    Johanes Holl and wife
to Carl Beber and wife is born a little daughter - 15 Mar 1794
    witness Kosina(?) Heinels
to Michael Lindenmuth and wife is born Ahel 1 Aug 1794 witness
    Jacob Zanger and wife
to Jacob Schuz and wife is born Jacob 3 Aug 1794 witness Jacob
    Zanger and wife
to Friedrich Nambach and wife is born Sophia 17 Aug 1793 witness
    Mathias Daut and wife
baptised (?) 14th:
to Georg Hofman and wife Barbara is born a little daughter witness
    Jacob Schutz and wife Elisabeth
baptised Jan 9th:
to Ludwig Schreyer and wife is born a little son - 10 Jan 17(94)
    witness the parents themselves
baptised Mar 8th:
to Adam Klein and wife is born a little daughter - 14 Oct 1794
    witness Maria Schmied
baptised Apr 9th:
to Philipp Kiester and wife is born Georg 27 Jan 179(4)
to Johanes Beber and wife is born Jacob 2 Jul 1794 witness Martin
    Wittmar and wife
to Peter Kiblinger and wife is born Elisabeth 2 Jul 1794 witness the
    widow Appolonia Kiblinger
to Johanes Kiblinger and wife Elisabeth is born Philipp 2 Aug 1794
    witness Peter Koch and wife
to Johanes (B?)aush and wife is born Georg 26 Oct 1794 witness
    Abraham and wife
to Michael (Bo?)singer and wife is born Elisabeth 26 Sep 1794
    witness Elisabeth Biecherin
to Johanes Klein and wife is born Chatrina 20 Jan 1796

1795
to Jacob Weyeand and wife is born Johanes 20 Apr 1794 witness
    Ulrich Seeler and wife Maria
to Daniel Schuz and wife Chatrina is born Barbara 4 Apr 1795
    witness Madlena Holire

to Johanes Maurer and wife is born Chatrina 23 Mar 1795 witness
Christoph Schmied and wife

to Andreas Schaefer and wife is born Christine 1 Mar 1795 witness
    Elisabeth Besinger

to Heinrich Dutweiler and wife is born Chatrina 1 Jun 1795 witness
    the parents themselves

baptised May 17th:

to Samuel Beber and wife Chatrina is born Valentin in Mar 1795
    witness Johan Beber and wife Anna

to Georg Zanger and wife is born Johanes Feb 1795 witness
    Leonhard Dutweiler and wife

to Christoph Venus and Maria Elisabeth Schram is born an
    illegitimate child Maria Barbara 21 Apr 1794 witness Heinrich
    Schulterman and wife Chatrina

baptised Jul 5th:

to Johan Kiblinger and wife Elisabeth is born Johanes 26 Mar 1795
    witness Mathias Willberger and wife

to Heinrich (L?)aub and wife Elisabeth is born Margreth 17 Jul 1794
    witness Matthias Willberger and wife

baptised (Jul) 26th:

to Philipp Hauert and wife is born Jonathan 15 Apr 1795 witness
    Matheis Aman and wife

baptised Aug 16th:

to Adam Hauert and wife Chatrina is born Elisabeth 8 Jun 1795
    witness Johan Adam Z(imerman?) and wife Elisabeth

baptised Jul 20th:

to Jacob Koch and wife is born Adam 29 Aug 1795 witness Adam
    Paulus and wife

[Page 17]
1795
baptised (?) 26th:

to Georg Koenig and wife is born Johanes 20 Jul 1795 witness
    Gottlieb Pfeifer and wife

to Peter Beb and wife is born Johanes 29 Aug 1794 witness Ulrich
    Seeler and wife Maria

baptised (?) 27th:

to Peter Braun and wife Elisabeth is born Peter 23 Aug 179. witness
    the parents themselves

to Johan Huttelloch and wife Elisabeth is born Jacob 29 Aug 1795 witness Ulrich Seeler and wife Anna Maria

baptised (?) 25th:

to Peter Kiester and wife Elisabeth is born Salome 6 Jul 1795
witness Christine Schreyer

to Johanes Martin and wife is born Jacobus in Jul 1795 witness
Valentin Schalle and wife Chatrina

baptised (?) 26th:

to Adam Paulus and wife is born Jacob 17 Sep 1795 witness Jacob
Koch and wife Elisabeth

1796

baptised Feb 21st:

to Philipp Boehmer and wife Elisabeth is born Johan Philipp 20 Jan
1796 witness the parents themselves

to Christian Hofman and wife Barbara is born Chatrina 24 Sep 1795
witness Leonhard Dutweiler and wife Chatrina

baptised (?) 28th:

to Jacob Dutweiler and wife Anna is born Maria 28 Oct 1795
witness Maria Dutweiler

baptised (?) 29th:

to Jacob Pott and wife Esther is born Chatrina 18 Feb 1796 witness
Adam Pott and wife Sabrina

baptised May 15th:

to Johanes Ehrly and wife (?) is born a daughter 23 Jan 1796
witness Wassel(?) Schmiedt and wife Angina and child was
named Kattarina

Johanes Bros(?) and wife Elisabeth is born a daughter 18 May 1796
witness Johanes Botdorf and wife Christina and the child's name
was Christina

[Page 18]

to Hannes (W?)ei(k?)er and wife Elisabeth a son named Johannes is
born 7 May 1796 baptised 19 Jun 1796 witness Johanes (4 words)

to Friedrich Schwartz and wife Anna Maria a son named Johannes
is born 29 Apr 1796 baptised 19 Jun witnesses were Abram Bohn
and Susanna

to Johannes Gabel and wife Elisabeth a son Wilhelm is born 5 Feb
1796 baptised 19 Jun 1796 witnesses were Jacob Schmidt and
parents

to Johannes (W?)erner and wife Elisabeth a daughter named
Elisabeth is born 22 Jan 1796 baptised 27 Jul 1796 witnesses
were g(rand?)mother, father and mother

to Paulus (B?)roos and wife Magdalena a son named Johannes is born 9 Jul 1796 baptised (4?) Aug 1796 Ulrich Scheryer and wife Elisabeth

to Conrad Klein and wife Maria a daughter named Sarah is born 25 Jan 1796 baptised 14 Aug 1796 witnesses were Christoph Schmidt and wife A(?)ngina

[Page 19]

to Jacob Schutz and wife a son named Michael is born 18 May 1796 baptised 11 Jul 1796 witnesses were mother and father of child

to Georg Bessinger and wife a son named Johannes is born 3 Aug 1796 baptised 11 Jul 1796(sic) witnesses were Peter Bessinger and wife

to Samuel Seiter and wife a daughter named Elisabeth is born 2 Apr 1796 baptised 11 Jul 1796 witnesses were Martin Ma..mar and wife

to Abraham Bruseis and wife a daughter named Sebrana(?) is born 12 Jul 1796 baptised 11 Jul 1796 (sic) witnesses were Johannes Schlossen and wife

to Johannes Weizel and wife a son named Peter is born 23 Jul 1796 baptised 11 Jul 1796 (sic) witnesses were Peter Strictlach(?) and wife

[Page 20]

to Ulrich Sehler and wife Maria a son named Mattheis is born 15 Aug 1796 baptised 9 Oct 1796 witnesses were Mattheiss Amen and wife Elisabeth

to Jacob Zech and wife Elisabeth a son named Jacob is born 4 Dec 1795 baptised 17 Apr 1796 witnesses were Georg Bees and wife Elisabeth

to Peter Besinger and wife Barbara a son named Valentin is born 9 Mar 1796 baptised 17 Apr 1796 witnesses were Stossel Schmidt and wife Lucina

to Jacob Kothaermel and wife Catherina a daughter named Catherina is born 14 Jul 1795 baptised 17 Apr 1796 witnesses were Adam Argobreiht and wife Barbara

to Johannes Schlosser and wife Elisabeth a son named Jacob is born 30 Nov 1796 baptised 1 Jan 1797 witness Jacob Schlosser

to Michael Bessinger and wife Barbara a son named Johannes is

born 26 Oct 1796 baptised 1 Jan 1797 witnesses were Johannes
Schmidt and wife Magdalena

[Page 21]
to Adam Klein and wife Susanna a daughter named Anna Maria is
    born 22 Nov 1796 baptised 29 Jan 1797 witnesses were Michael
    Ehrman and wife Anna Maria
to Jacob Koch and wife Catherina a daughter named Catherina
    Elisabeth is born 29 Nov 1796 baptised 29 Jan 1797 witness
    Susanna Sehlerin
to Ludwig Keller and wife Gertraut a daughter named Anna
    Catherina is born 6 Nov 1796 baptised 26 Mar 1797 witnesses
    were the parents
to Johannes Batdorf and wife Christina a son named Simon is born
    20 Dec 1796 baptised 26 Mar 1797 witnesses were the parents
to Johannes Holl and wife Anna Maria a daughter named Susanna
    is born 10 Oct 1796 baptised 16 Apr 1797 witnesses were the
    parents
to Frantz Ott and wife Catherina a son named Jacob is born 5 Jan
    1797 baptised 23 Apr 1797 witnesses were Friedrich Schwartz
    and wife Anna Maria

[Page 22]
to Abraham Hoffman and wife Dorothea a son named Friedrich is
    born 3 Nov 1796 baptised 23 Apr 1797 witnesses were Valentin
    and wife Anna Maria
to Peter Besinger and wife Hana a son named Heinrich is born 14
    Jan 1797 baptised 23 Apr 1797 witnesses were Ulrich Sehler and
    wife Anna Maria
to Adam Lang and wife Sal(ome?) a child is born 27 Oct baptised 27
    Apr
to Peter Zolar and wife Eva a son named Johannes is born 27 Oct
    1796 baptised 30 Apr 1797 witnesses were Heinrich Seib and
    wife
to Peter Bed and wife Maria a daughter named Feronica is born 11
    Nov 1796 baptised 30 Apr 1797 witness Elisabeth Unruh

[Page 23]
to Georg Hoffman and wife Barbara a daughter named Catherina is
    born 21 Jan 1797 baptised 30 Apr 1797 witnesses were the
    parents

to Salomon Hossman and wife Elisabeth a son named Johannes is
     born 21 Dec 1796 baptised 21 May 1797 witnesses were Daniel
     Duentel and wife Susanna
to Johannes Duentel and wife Christina a son named Daniel is born
     1 Jan 1797 baptised 21 May 1797 witnesses were Ludwig
     Schreyer and wife Anna Maria
to Georg Elye and wife Elisabeth a son is born 12 Feb 1797 baptised
     21 May 1797 witnesses were Friedrich Schwartz and wife Anna
     Maria
to Johannes Huttloch and wife Elisabeth a daughter named
     Susanna is born 5 Feb 1797(?) baptised 21 May 1797 witness
     child's grandmother Anna Maria Sehlerin

[Page 24]
to Philipp Kraft and wife Barbara a son named Jacob is born 16 Oct
     1797 baptised 28 May 1797 witness Heinrich Berkyeider
to Georg Heind and wife Elisabeth a son named Jacob is born 16
     Apr 1797 baptised 28 May 1797 witness Jacob Kesler and wife
     Catherina
to Heinrich Daub and wife Magdalena a son named Joseph is born
     20 Oct 1796 baptised 28 May 1797 witnesses Wilhelm Trorbach
     and wife Catherina
to Joh: (R?)ausch and wife Magdalena a daughter named Elisabeth
     is born 13 Jan 1797 baptised 3 Jun 1797 witnesses were Adam
     Pott and wife Catherina
to Joh. Schmidt and wife Magdalena a son named Jacob is born 20
     Apr 1797 baptised 21 Jun 1797 witnesses were Christoph
     Schmidt and wife Catrina
to Adam Schmeltzer and wife Maria Sonia a son named Joseph is
     born 27 Nov 1794 baptised 4 Jun 1797 witnesses the parents

[Page 25]
to Joh: Maurer and wife Elisabeth a daughter named Susanna is
     born 13 Feb 1797 baptised 4 Jun 1797 witness Adam Klein and
     wife Susanna
          Anno 1797

Names of Parents   Names of children and baptism date
     Godparents witnessing baptism

Daniel Hoffman & Magdalena | Moses born 18 Jun 1797
Joh: Beder and wife Anna
Johannes Mildenberger & Anna | Jacob born 2 Aug 1796
  bap.4 Jun 1797 | parents themselves
Joh. Graeh and wife Catherina | Magdalena b.6 Mar 1797
  bap.9 Jul 1797 | Christoph and wife Catrina their marks
Jacob Zech and wife Elisabeth | Catherina b.17 Jun 1797 bap.23 Jul
  1797 | Catherina Beckin
Franz K(?)arth and wife Dorothea | Abraham b.17 May 1797 bap.23
  Jul 1797 | parents themselves
Georg Koenig and wife Magdalena | Margreth b.12 Apr 1797
  bap.23 Jul 1797 | Georg Klemmer and wife Magdalena
In the year 1796 to Mrs. Magdalena named hereafter a son is born
  12 Nov baptised 30 Jan 1797 witnesses were Jacob Schuetz and
  wife Elisabeth
In the year 1796 to Peter Schuetz and wife So....(?) a child named
  Johannes is born baptised 30 Jun 1797 witness was Jacob
  Schuetz and wife Elisabeth

[Page 26]
       Anno 1797

Names of Parents   Names of children and baptism date
    Godparents witnessing baptism

In the year 1796 23 Oct to Philib Schuetz and wife Chatrina a
  daughter named Elisabaeth is born baptised 30 Jan 1797
  witnesses were father and mother
Jacob Argobreiht & wife Anna Maria | Johannes b.Jun 1797 bap.3
  Aug 1797 | Friedrich Schwartz and wife Anna Maria
Michael Stambach and wife Magdalena | Maria b.20 Apr 1797
  bap.13 Aug
Jacob Schenk and wife Catherina | Susana b.20 May bap.12
  Aug | Michael Weis and wife
Georg Lang and wife Susana | Jacob b.8 Jul bap.13 Aug
  | Jacob Kesster and wife Catherina
Paul Heucolye and wife Catherina | Johannes b.6 May 1797
  Christin b.same bap.27 Aug 1797 | Daniel and Joh. Duendel
Joh. Berkye and wife Elisabeth | Sarah b.31 Jul 1797 bap.10
  Sep 1797 | Heinrich Berkye and wife Eva

Daniel Fascher and wife Anna | Andreas b.27 Oct 1796 bap 10 Sep
    1797 | Jacob Wilberger and wife Eva

[Page 27]
to Peter Weizel and wife Maria a son named Johannes is born 28 Jul
    1797 baptised 10 Sep 1797 witnesses Ludwig Keller and wife
    Gertraut
to Abraham Zanger and wife Catherina a son named Friedrich is
    born 13 Aug 1797 baptised 24 Sep 1797 witnesses the parents
to Daniel Schuetz and wife Catherina a daughter named Elisabeth
    is born 5 Aug 1797 baptised 24 Sep 1797 witnesses Heinrich
    Schulterman and wife Catherina
to Georg Zanger and wife a daughter named Susanna B..oman is
    born 22 Jun 1797 baptised 8 Oct
to Heinrich Schneider and wife Maria a daughter named Susanna is
    born 9 Aug 1797 baptised 22 Oct 1797 witnesses Adam Klein and
    wife Susanna
to Heinrich Braut and wife (rest of line) born 5 Jul 1797 (rest of line)
    (3 or 4 lines)

[Page 28]
to Johan Koch and wife a son named Jeremias is born 13 Oct 1797
    baptised 3 Dec 1797
to Johannes Pabel and wife a daughter named Susana is born 25
    Oct 1797 baptised 3 (?) 1797
to Gottlob Pfeiffer a son named Jacob is born 28 Oct 1797 baptised
    13 Jan 1798 witnesses Jacob Zanger and wife
to Peter Kister a daughter named Magdalena is born 22 Nov 1797
    baptised 11 Apr 1798 witness Ludwig Schunger and wife
to Jacob Dindel a daughter named Leise is born 16 Nov 1804
    baptised and witnessed by Friedrich Dindel and wife
to Johannes Bross a daughter named Stromor is born 8 Jan 1809
    baptised and witnessed by father and mother

[Page 29]
to Peter Behsinger and wife a son named Peter is born 18 Feb 1798
    baptised 25 Mar 1798
to Peter Kiepfler and wife a daughter named Susanna is born 16 Oct
    1797 baptised 9 Apr
to Jacob Wilberger and wife Catherina a daughter is born 4 Mar
    1798 baptised 6 May 1798

to Georg Had and wife a son named Johannes is born 29 Aug 1797
   baptised 6 May 1798
to Abraham Beosirs and wife a daughter named Anna is born 14
   Feb 1798 baptised 6 May 1798
to Hannes Broos and wife a daughter named Magdalena is born 21
   Dec 1797 baptised 6 May 1798
to Georg Chrig a son named Johannes is born 18 Oct 1798 baptised
   6 May 1798

[Page 30]
to Johannes Leiter and wife a daughter named Maria is born 29
   Mar 1798 baptised 29 May 1798

[Page 31]
to Martin Wittmer and wife a son named Johannes is born 31 Aug
   1797 baptised 27 May 1798

[Page 32]
to Jacob Schmeltzer and wife a daughter named Maria is born 23
   Mar 1798 baptised 27 May 1798
to Georg Ernst and wife a daughter named Annamaria is born 9 Oct
   1797 baptised 8 Jul 1798
to Petter Brann and wife a daughter named Christina is born 19
   May 1798 baptised 8 Jul 1798
to Abraham Weitzel and wife a son named Wilhelm is born 23 Mar
   1798 baptised 8 Jul 1798
to Georg Rauten and wife Elisabeth two sons named Johannes and
   Jacob are born 2 Jun 1798 baptised 5 Aug 1798
to Jacob Haelluenger and wife a daughter named Annamarie is born
   3 Jul 1798 baptised 5 Aug 1798
to Adam Schnietzer and wife Maria a son named Johan Georg is
   born 3 Jul 1798 baptised 5 Aug 1798

[Page 33]
to Jacob Schuetz and wife a son named Johannes is born 18 May
   1798 baptised 5 Aug 1798
to Hannes Weidig and wife a son named Joseph is born 12 May 1798
   baptised 2 Feb 1798
to Heinrich Jutzler and wife a daughter named Elisabeth is born 23
   May 1798 baptised 2 Sep 1798

to Johannes Hetrich and wife a son named Jacob is born 21 Aug baptised 2 Sep 1798

to Adam Meye and wife a son named Adam is born 1 May 1798 baptised 2 Sep 1798

to Hannes Herrendon and wife a son named Daniel is born 9 Apr 1798 baptised 2 Sep 1798

to Adam Argobreiht and wife a daughter named Salmye is born 13 Jun 1798 baptised 2 Sep 1798

[Page 34]

to Conrad Klein a son is born 17 Aug 1798 baptised 29 Sep witnesses were Peter Kessler and wife

to Adam Hauss and wife a daughter Margreda is born 19 Jan 1798 baptised 30 Sep 1798

to Georg Kehrbach and wife a son named Jacob is born 12 Jul 1798 baptised 30 Sep 1798

to Hannes Maesserye and wife a daughter named MariElisabeth is born 16 Aug 1798 baptised 30 Sep 1798

to Jacob Koch and wife a daughter named Barbara is born 26 Aug 1798 baptised 30 Sep 1798

to Georg Kerff and wife a son named Johannes is born 6 Jul 1798 baptised 30 Sep 1798

tp Adam Baulus and wife a daughter named Anna is born 2 Jul 1798 baptised 30 Sep 1798

[Page 35]

to Heinrich Ded and wife a daughter named Margreda is born 1 Apr 1798 baptised 8 Jul 1798

to Johannes Duendel and wife a daughter named Susana is born 7 Aug 1798 baptised 28 Oct 1798

to Adam Bott and wife a daughter named Susana is born 17 Sep 1798 baptised 28 Oct 1798

to Ulrich (Kn?)eins and wife a son named Valentin is born 2 Aug 1798 baptised 25 Nov 1798

to Fridrich Schwartz and wife a son named Fridrich is born 30 Sep 1798 baptised 29 Nov 1798

to Martin Bad and wife a son named Jacob is born 17 Oct 1798 baptised 25 Nov 1798

to Heinrich Lauh and wife a son named Jacobus is born 6 May 1798 baptised 25 Sep 1798

[Page 36]
To David Wilberger and wife a son named Johannes is born 30 Oct
    1798 baptised 25 Nov 1798
to Johannes Herry and wife a son named David is born 31 Sep
    baptised 20 Jan 1799 witness Johannes Seeler
to Johannes Schwartz a son named Jacob is born 24 Dec 1798
    baptised 17 Feb 1799 witnesses Hannes Maserlye
to Jacob Herner and wife a son named Heinrich is born 6 Jan 1799
    baptised 14 Apr 1799
to Caspar Boesinger and wife a son named Hannes is born 15 Feb
    1799 baptised 14 Apr 1799
to Jacob Schmiedt and wife a son named Michael is born 20 Nov
    1798 baptised 14 Apr 1799

[Page 37]
to Wilhelm Schanfer and wife a son named Wilhelm is born 11 Sep
    1798 baptised 14 Apr 1799
to Hannes Schreier and wife a daughter named Cathrina is born 28
    Nov 1798 baptised 14 Apr
to Jacob Herl and wife a daughter named Annamaria is born 6 Sep
    1798 baptised 14 Apr 1799
to Frantz Ott and wife a daughter named Annamaria is born 5 Apr
    1799 baptised 11 May 1799
to Jacob Zech and wife a daughter named Elisabeth is born 28 Oct
    1798 baptised 12 May 1799
to Petter Bosinger and wife a daughter named Susanna is born 26
    Mar 1799 baptised 12 May 1799

[Page 38]
to Salomon Hoffman and wife a son named Samuel is born 29 Nov
    1798 baptised 12 May 1799
to Hannes Koch and wife a daughter named Elisabeth is born 17
    Jan 1799 baptised 12 May 1799
to Hannes Maurer and wife a daughter named Sara is born 13 Apr
    1799 baptised 12 May 1799
to Georg Boesinger and wife a daughter named Elisabeth is born 13
    Aug 1798 baptised 12 May 1799
to Urbanes Hoeffner and wife a son named Johannes is born 15 Oct
    1798 baptised 12 May 1799

to Hannes Ergenbreih and wife a son named Ludwig is born 17 Jun 1798 baptised 12 May 1799

[Page 39]

to Carl Weber and wife a daughter named Annamaria is born 18 Dec 1798 baptised 12 May 1799

to Heinrich Neher and Elisabeth - Catherina is born 26 Jun 1799 baptised 9 Jun 1799 witnesses Heinrich Schulter and wife Catherina

to Matthia Koginger(?) and Elisabeth - S(usana?) is born 10 Dec 1796 baptised 9 Jun 1799 witness Susana Holbisen

to Martin Koginger and Elisabeth - Jacob is born 28 Jul 1798 baptised 9 Jun 1799 witnesses Jacob Schneider and wife

to Adam Klein and wife Susana - Catharina is born 11 Apr 1799 baptised 7 Jul 1799 witness Catharina Broch

to Peter Zollar and wife Eva - Petter is born 26 Apr 179. baptised 7 Jul 1799 witnesses Heinrich Seihs and wife Susana

to Johannes Scholl and wife A. Maria - Anna is born 8 Nov 1798 baptised 4 Aug 1799 witnesses father and mother

to Michael Boesinger and wife Barbara - Jos. Jacob is born 29 May 1799 baptised 4 Aug 1799 witnesses Jacob Scho.(?) and wife Elisabeth

to Heinrich Stud(?) and wife Christina - (?)Struniediss(?) is born 9 May 1799 baptised 4 Aug 1799 witnesses Georg Glinnus(?) and wife Magdalena

to Peter Maizel and wife Maria - Jacob is born 11 Apr 1799 baptised 4 Aug 1799 witnesses Johannes Seeler (single) and Katherina Tuferweiler (single)

to Johannes Schmidt and wife Magdalena - Johannes is born 13 Jun 1799 baptised 11 Aug 1799 witnesses Johannes Schole and wife Lucina

to Abraham Hoffman and wife Dorothea - (Johannes?) is born 21 May 1799 baptised 4 Aug 1799 witnesses David Dindel and wife Susanna

[Page 40]

to Adam Lag and wife Magdalena - Blias(?) is born 9 Apr 1799 baptised 31 Aug 1799 witnesses Ulrich Seeler and wife Susanna

to Johannes Widmar and wife Elisabeth - David is born 31 Jan 1799 baptised 31 Aug 1799 witness father and mother

to Georg Baust and wife Barbara - Elisabeth is born 3 Jun 1799
baptised 31 Aug 1799 witness Elisabeth Ott
to Friedrich Fenchel and wife Magdalena - Johannes is born 4 Aug
1799 baptised 31 Aug 1799 witnesses Daniel Dendel and wife
Susanna
to Philip Kister and wife Catherina - Susanna is born 4 Aug 1799
baptised 1 Sep 1799 witness Catherina Schlossern (single)
to Stuf(?) Griger and wife Barbra - Georg is born 29 Sep 1799
baptised 8 Aug witnesses father and mother
to Georg Lang and wife Susana - Sara is born 29 Sep 1799 baptised
30 Jul 1799(sic) witness Catherina Schlosser (single)
to Johannes Keller and wife Susana - Catherina is born 29 Sep 1799
baptised 2 Aug 1799(sic) witness Elisabeth Keller
to Jos. Bross and wife Elisabeth - Sara is born 29 Sep 1799 baptised
30 Jul 1799(sic) witnesses father and mother
to Jos. Frieden and wife Elsi - Philip is born 29 Sep 1799 baptised 25
Dec 1799 witnesses Heinrich Kessler and wife Barbara
to Johannes Rausch and wife Magdalena - Sara is born 22 Feb 1799
baptised 27 Oct 1799 witness Sara Rausch
to Heinrich Fillinger and wife Elisabeth - Jacob is born (?) baptised
27 Oct 1799 witness Jacob Hudloch
to Johannes Bentz and wife Anna Maria - Anna Maria is born 17 Jul
1799 baptised 27 Oct 1799 witness Elisabeth Bentzen 1800
to Ulrich Sehler and wife Maria - Anna Maria is born 27 Oct
baptised 20 Apr witnesses Johannes Herry and wife Elisabeth
to Jacob Banger and wife Margretha - Heinrich is baptised 20 Apr
witnesses Heinrich Kesler and wife Barbara
to Martin Bod and wife Maria - Michael is born 24 Jan baptised 20
Apr 1800 witnesses Martin Bod and wife Maria
to Edwadt Rohlar and wife Magdalena - Susana is born 3 Jan
baptised 20 Apr witnesses Johannes Rohlar and wife Susana

[Page 41]
to Georg Rauterbush and wife Elisabeth - Annamaria is born 1. Jan
baptised 20 Apr witnesses Annamaria Rauterbush
to Barbra Sehlern - Sara and Wilhelm are born 8 and 9 May 1799
baptised 20 Apr witnesses Georg Braun and wife Barbara
to Jacob Schutz - Elisabeth is born 4 Apr baptised 1 Jun witness
Catherina Huensern

to Martin Stembach - Michal Stembach is born 1 Aug baptised 22
Jun(sic) witnesses Michal Stembach and wife

to Johannes Uterbor - Christina Uterbor is born 3 Dec baptised 22
Jun witness Christina Zingern

to Jacob Haisman and Elisabeth - Jacob is born 17 Mar baptised 3
Aug witness Petter Koch and Annamaria

to Martin Wittmer and wife Elisabetha - Elisabeth is born 3 Dec
1799 baptised 17 Aug witnesses Daniel Sua...(?) and wife
Elisabeth

to Johannes Duendel and wife Christina - Selmye is born 25 (?)
baptised 26 Oct witness Daniel Duendel

[Page 42]

to Wilhelm Gaul and Barbara - Johannes is born 30 Apr 1799
baptised 8 Nov 1800 witnesses parents

to Peter Hessen - Maria is born (?) Sep 1800 baptised 8 Nov
witnesses Jodrel Fe.....(?) and Anna

to Johannes Braunn - Jodel is born 30 Jan 1800 baptised 8 Nov
witnesses Peter Kes(ler?) and Catherina

to Jodel Willberger and Eva - Jodel is born 13 Jul 1800 baptised 9
Nov 1800 witnesses Jodul Sch....(?) and wife

(4 lines)

to Johan Kiebler(?) and Catherina - Elisabeth is born 21 Sep 1800
baptised 1 Feb 1801 witnesses mothers sign (2 words)

to Heinrich Sar(?) and Elisabeth - Susanna is born 24 Aug 1800
baptised 1 Feb 1801 witnesses father and mother

to Konrad Delen(?) and Maria - Catherina is born 18 Sep 1800
baptised 1 Feb 1801 witness Catherina Sehler

to Daniel Schutz and Elisabeth - Jadul is born 6 Dec 1800 baptised 1
Mar 1801 witness Jadul Sch....(?) and Elisabeth

to Johan Sehle(?) and Maria - Catherina is born 12 Aug 1801
baptised 24 May witnesses parents

to Peter Braun and Elisabeth - (D,X?)ebeda(?) is born 20 Jan 1801
baptised 24 May witnesses Peter Kab....(?) and wife

to Gad; Goat(?) and Elisabeth - Herichs Catherina is born 9 Mar
baptised 26 May 1801 witnesses the parents

to Heinrich Schneider and Maria Flie(?) - Joh. Georg is born 2(?) Oct
and Anne Maria is born 3 Oct both baptised May witnesses Johs.
Schn. (3-4 words)

ST. MICHAEL'S UNION
(Reformed only after 1802)

(1st page)
To Peter Lam and Catherina 24 Oct 1794 and baptised Mar 1796
to Johannes Daur (and wife) a daughter is born 26 Apr 1795 and
    named Anna M(aria?)
to Maria Magdalena a daughter is born 14 Jul 1795 baptised 22 Nov
    1795 witness (?) (?) (?)
(large X drawn through the above information)
In the budget of St(?) (Michaels?) (?) (?) (2 lines?)
From(?) In the Colecte (7 words?)
(7 words ?)

Parents(religion) Baptism date	Names of child	Birthdate
Philip Leimand(?) Lutheran 19 Jul 1801	Philip Konrad(?)	22 Nov 1800
Andreas Scram - Lutheran 19 Jul 1801	Abraham	11 Jan 1801
Friederich Miller - Reformed 19 Jul 1801	Salomier	7 May 1801
Georg Ifrich - Reformed 19 Jul 1801	Elisabeth	6 Nov 1800
Philip Haus(?) - Barbara 19 Jul 1801	Susanna	10 Sep 1800
Adam Shraf(?)	Elisabeth	30 Jun 1791
Joh. Herzog(?) - Lutheran 10 Mar 1792	Sara	6 Jan 1792
Adam Schraff(?)	Elisabeth	30 Jun 1791
Joh. Weis - Lutheran 13 May 1794	Johan Michael	1793

(next page)

Names of Child Witnesses	Birthdate	Baptism date
Jonathan Johan Eteis and Catherina	7 Mar 1800	14 Sep 1800

Catherine   16 Aug 1799   14 Sep 1800
   parents
Samuel   9 Jan 1799   14 Sep 1800
   Georg Schuyler and Elisabeth
Johannes   29 Nov 1799(?) 14 Sep 1800
   Daniel Iman.. and childs mother
Philipp   .. Jan 1800   14 Sep 1800
   parents
Willhelm   24 Jul(?) 1796   14 Mar 1794
Anna Maria   23 Aug 1798   28 Mar 1799
Maria Magdalena   24 Jun 1795   .. Mar 1796
   Elies: (2 words) Georg Siestela his wife Maria
Elisabeth   7 Oct 1801   .. (?) 1801
   Fried. Mueler and Elisa. Mueler (3 lines)

TRINITY LUTHERAN CHURCH

Names of Parents Baptised	of Children	Born
Johanes Breit and wife Anna	Kinirmer(?)	3 Mar 1798
Johanes Breit and wife Anna	Jacob	12 May 1799
Johanes Breit and wife Anna	Dalila Rigney	16 Nov 1800
Johanes Breit and wife Anna	Carrolina	16 May 1802
Johanes Breit and wife Anna	Cohlman	9 Apr 1808
Johanes Breit and wife Anna	Janeany	19 Jan 1806
Johanes Breit and wife Anna	Druesilla	1 Oct 1809
Johanes Breit and wife Anna	Charlot	30 Jul 1811
Johanes Breit and wife Anna	Marshal	20 Feb 18..(?)

(next page)
Names of the (2 words)

1. Mr. Friedrichruet
2. Mr.
3. Madg. Mueller
4. Johan Laide
5. Mrs.
6. Mr. Millr.
7. Mrs.
8. Ledi Daufe
9. Mal Bolde
10. Mrs.
11. David Bolin
12. Mr. Bolde
13. Braber...(?)
14. J. Keefer
15. and wife
16. Ad(am?) Fogt
17. and wife
18. Cath. Fogt
19. (?) Fogt
20. Elis(abeth) Fogt
21. Ad.. Fogt
22. and wife
23. Joh. S..f(?)
(1 line)

27. Stohfel(?) E....(?)
28. Franz E....(?)
29. Heinz C....(?)
30. (?) E(lisabeth?)
31. Sara(?) Elisabeth(?)
32. Joh. Du....(?)
33. Johan L...t(?)
34. Adam (?)
35. Joh. Seiber
36. Phil Miller
37. Molly (?)
38. Lowe(?) (?)
39. Elisabeth(?) Sch.....(?)
40. E...(?) Heinz
41. Catharine (?)
42. Mar(ia?) (H?)of...(?)
43. Ev..(?) Dorf(?)
44. Bar(bara) D..ste
45. Anna Diete(?)
46. Polly S.....tina
47. Hana Schoehm(?)
48. Chri...(?) Debo...(?)
49. Ana Fogt

SMITH'S CREEK/LINVILLE CREEK BAPTIST CHURCH
(later BROCK'S GAP BAPTIST CHURCH)

Excerpts from the minutes

The congregation met alternately at a meeting house on Smith's
Creek and at one on Linville Creek. In 1774 Smith's Creek Church
was constituted as an independant congregation. Linville Creek
Church continued. For a more detailed account of the minutes,
1756-1844, see John W. Wayland's Virginial Valley Records, pp. 48-
84.

Covenant or constitution signed by John Alderson, Jane Alderson,
Samuel Newman, Martha Newman, John Harrison, William Castle
Berry, and Margaret Castle Berry. These persons and John Thomas
who had been baptized before and his brother James Thomas who
was baptized the day after constitution formed the body of the
church. Rees Thomas and Mary States belonging to churches in
Pennsylvania were admitted.

"Samuel Newman and his wife, being Members of Montgomery
Church, in the county of Philadelphia, was the first Members of any
Baptist Church that settled here. But in some small time after he
was setled, John Harrison senior, being convinced of his Duty to
come to the holy Ordinance of Baptism, went for it somewhere
towards New York to a Place called Oyster-Bay, but was received
then a Member of no particular Church, But by a Certificate of his
Baptism, was recommended to be received, or associated into any
Church of that Order ... In all this While, there was no Minister of
that Denomination came here. The next Family of that
Denomination, (whereof the Head was a Member.) was Rees
Thomas and he setled on Linvils Creek. The next Member was a
Sister, viz. Mary Newman the Wife of Jonathan Newman, belonging
to the Church of Christ in Southamton, in the county of Bucks; as
Rees Thomas belonged to the Church of the same Order in Cumry
Township, Lancaster County. About this Time Mr. Samuel Eaton
(the first Baptist Minister in Order.) visited these Parts, and
preached at old Mr. Harrisons, the only Disciplle he knew to be in
the Place. The next in Order was Mr. Benjamin Griffith, who came
on purpose to visit the Aforesaid Brother Samuel Newman. The
next after him ws our Reverend Brother whom God at last was

pleased to send as his Instrument, to settle this Church.

"His first Visit was to Rees Thomas, and on Linvils Creek, The Forest, and North River, where the People were much affected, and prepared to receive further instructions from his Mouth. The next in Order was again Mr. Samuel Eaton, he visited only the inhabitants of Smiths Creek.

"Then God was pleased to visit the Inhabitants of Smiths Creek, Linvils Creek, and North River of Shenandoah, (the Places where now the Church is built,) by Mr. John Gano, (a faithful Servant of his,) who was recieved by the Love and Likeing, of almost all sorts of People. After him the Revrd Mr Alderson, visited again his second Time, and then began to concluded tom come and Settle, and bought Land, and then came, and through the Grace of God, was instrumental in gathering the Church, by whom also She was constituted, and the first Pastor of the Church of Christ, at Smiths and Linvils Creeks, in Frederick and Augusta County's, as in the Covenant afore written specifield. Thus was the Labours of those Gentlemen aforenamed, for the Space of Eleven Years, from the First Setler, as above named, and about one Yar before the Constitution of the Church. William Castle Berry and his Wife, came and setled on Muddy Creek, in Augusta County, being both Members of Newbritain Church, and of these were the Church at first Built. And others there were none, till gathered by the preaching of the Word, whereof was only two, which was added to the Church at the first Commuin, as hath been already related. Our Revrt Pastor Mr John Alderson, and Mrs Jane Alderson his wife being both Members of Newbritain Church in the County of Bucks, move their Residence, and came to us the same Spring before we were Constituted &c.

....

"At a general Meeting held in October 1756, by the three congregational Churches of Christ, baptis'd on personal Profession of Faith, in Fairfax & Frederick Counties, in Virginia,, it was agreed that the sd. churches, do Annually Meet at some one of their several Meeting-Houses, to hold Communion and Fellowship together, on the second Sabbath of June in each year hereafter, to begin with the Church of Christ at Smiths Creek in June the Second Sabbath 1757.

"The next Members that was added, was Mary Barrot, the Wife of Authur Barrot, she being brought up in Quakerism, (and being ignorant even of a morral Life, which they profess:) was convinced by a Sermon preached in the Begining of the year 1757 ... was received in April 1757. ...

"The next was Catherine Harrison, the wife of Jeremiah Harrison ... received a Member ... May 1757. ...

"The next Communion was held the 2d. Sabbath in June 1757, by Appointment of the three Churches above sd. in Annual Meeting, where was present with our Rev. Brother Mr Alderson, the Rev. Mr John Garrot, (Minister of the Church of Christ, of the same Faither and Gospel Order, with us, in Fairfax County, and likewise of Mill creek in Frederick County.) which two carryed on the solemn Publick Worship of God three Days successivly, in which Time the following Persons gave Obedience to the Commands of God, in his Gospel Ordinance of Baptism, and Laying on of Hands, and was received Members of ye Church of Christ, at the North River of Shannandoah, and Linvils Creek. The first was the Wife of George Nicholas: (She was a Presbyterian, and zealous in their Cause ...). The other a Gentleman of no mean Character, a Man in Authority both civil and military, Cornelious Ruddell, by Name ... formerly by Profession, a Church of England Man &c. This was our Fourth Communion since Constitution, at which Time they sd. three Churches mutually agreed, That the next yearly Meeting should be held with the Church of Christ at Catockton in Fairfax County, at the Time before appointed viz. the Second Sabbath in June 1758.

...

"At a Monthly Meeting th eDay before the Second Sabbath in August [1758] Mary Denham, the Wife of Joseph Denham offered herself to the Church and proposed for Baptism, upon which she was examined, and made a good & clear Confession of the Faith of the Gospel. (though she had been brought up a Quaker) ...

"After this Time, the Spring coming on, the Indian Troubles continued, and all Oppertunities of Meetings were taken from us, and not only so, but the whole Neighbourhood forced either to go into Forts or over the Mountains, to escape their Rage, in the Month of June following.

"At this Time [September 1759] there were two Members added viz. Jeremiah Ozban, & Mary Ozban his Wife, and all our Members were together save two: one by Reason of Distance and Cumber; the other disobedient and disorderly, refused to come, who having walked disorderly & riotous, was by the Church set aside, and not to be allowed Communion, nor any Act as a Member thereof, till Satisfaction given, viz. Cornelious Ruddell."

The next Communion [the 10th since formation of the Church] was delayed until 10 Aug 1760 becaues of "the Difficulty of Winter, the Troubles of removing back from our Flights, caused by the Enemy, and great Affliction of the Small-Pox raging in the Land."

At the fourth Sabbath of May 1761 Phillip Fegans was received. Five persons baptized: Thomas Porter , Jeremiah Harrison, John Ozban and his wife Elizabeth Ozban, Esther North wife of John North, the said North having been baptized elsewhere, Sarah Thomas wife of James Thomas, who already was a member.

On the second Sabbath of May 1762 Sarah Porter wife of Thomas Porter was received.

On Saturday, before the Second Sabbath of August [1762] Thomas George and his wife were baptized.

On 26 May 1764 an acount of abuse of Sister Jane Rodgers was given, a member of the Church at Cumm in Berks County, Pennsylvania, the abuse given by her son-in-law, Thomas Evans. A letter was to be sent to that Church.

20 April 1765 - Samuel Newman and his wife Martha, planning to move to North or South Carolina, were granted letters of dismission; also a letter of dismisson for Phillip Fegans to same place or places; also a letter for Mary Barrot who is by her Husband moved away.

Second Sabbath of June [1765] - Added two members, Joseph

Thomas and a Negro man called Joe.

Second Sabbath of August - added members, John Ray and Thomas Evans; admitted into transient Communion a person of Quality, viz., Silas Hart.

Second Sabbath in April 1766 - Nicholas Pain [Fain?] received into transient Communion, and Joseph Thomas excommunicated for scandalizing of a young Woman.

Third Sabbath in May 1766 - Silas Hart received into full Commuiion by a letter from Penypack Church in Pennsylvania.

Third Sabbath in June 1766 - Baptized Benjamin Alderson and his wife Ann.

Last Sabbath July 1766 - Grace Lockard wife of Daniel Lockard baptized.

Last Sabbath Aug [1766] - Ann Mace baptized.

Last Saturday May 1768 - Thos. Porter was appointed to warn Jno. Ray to appear before the Church to give Satisfaction for some offences and Mr Jno. Alderson to warn Jno. North to appear and that James Thomas should warn Jno. Thomas to appear at the Meeting House on Smiths Creek, the last Saturday in June next.

Last Saturday June 1768 - Jno. Ray was censured.

1st Saturday March 1769 - John Alderson, Jr., baptized.

1771 - Baptized Isaac Morris and his wife Ruth, Samuel Nicholas and Curtis Alderson.

1772 - Baptized Mary Henton wife of Evan Henton, Ann Needham wife of Jno. Needham, Hester Wright, ---, Susannah Ray wife of Jno. Ray, and Mary Alderson wife of Jno. Alderson Junior. Received into the Church: David Pergrin and his wife Mary being dismissed from the Great Valley Church in Pennsylvania and Thomas Woolsey being dismissed from a Church in New York Government and now ordained for the Ministry by order of this Church by Rev. Mr. Jno. Alderson.

Saturday, 8 Aug 1772 - Baptized Andrew Davison, Hannah Alderson wife of Thomas Alderson, Hannah Harrison wife of Jno. Harrison, Ann Dedrage, and Catherine Waren wife of Timothy Waren.

Brother David Pergrin to warn Thomas Evans to appear at next meeting to give his reason why he hath absented himself from Church.

Second Sabbath Aug 1773 - Thomas Woolsey and Ruth Morris to be dismissed. Inquiries to be made to the following persons as to their absences from Church: Silas Hart, Esther North wife of Jno. North. Isaac Morris to be dismissed by letter to the Church at Great Bethel.

6 Aug 1774 - Met together the members of church, living on Smiths Creek in order to examine into an affair between Jno. Conner and Susannah Ray wife of Jno. Ray. She stated that he had twice made known to her that he had lain under a temptation to have carnal conversation with her, but that he was delivered from under it, and a third time "he had made an Attact, which she utterly denied."

13 Aug 1774 - Jno. Conner was suspended of having any Church priviledge because of his unsemmly behaviour with Sister Sarah Porter and Sister Sarah Porter was suspended because of her unseemly behaviour with Jno. Conner. Esther North wife of Jno. North was suspended for inconstancy. Jno. Alderson, Sr., was suspended for reason of unseemly behaviour with a woman in Maryland.

Saturday Nov 1775 - Baptized Jno. Needham and Ann Bland.

10 May 1775 - Sarah Porter excommunicated.

Big Spring, 9 Nov 1776 - Jno. Ray and Jno. Conner excommunicated.

7 Dec 1776 - Abraham Elger received.

2nd Saturday Aug 1776 - Ann Mace to be continued as a member. Jno. Ray continued suspended.

13 March 1777 - Accompt of Revd. Jno. Alderson, sen., giving grounds to hope that the Lord hath restored him by a sound repentance, and was received into his place in the Church.

.... [No entries for 10 years] ...

15 Dec 1787 at house of Brother Jno. Lincoln - Anderson Moffett chosen as moderator and Jno. Thomas as clerk.

Saturday before third Sabbath, Feb 1788, at the house of Zebulon Harrison - Word to be sent to Silas Hart and James Thomas and his wife acquainting them of our next Church Meeting.

2nd Sabbath in April 1788 - Mary Lincoln, wife of Jno. Lincoln offered a short experience. Brother Jno. Runyan to be invited to officiate as Deacon at next Communion.

3rd Sabbath in May 1788 - James Thomas and his wife Sarah were given letter of dismission to join another Church of the same faith and order. Baptized Mary Lincoln.

2nd Sabbath in Sep 1788 - John Lockard received into Fellowship.

Saturday before 2nd Sabbath April 1789 - To write to John Stinson, supposedly legally baptized, asking him to join the church. To seek a greater intercourse and reciprocal union and communion with our sister church on Smith's Creek.

5th Sabbath in Nov 1789 - James Ireland present to administer sacrament.

2nd Sabbath in May 1790 - David Thomas acted as moderator. Margaret Thomas, dau. of Evan Thomas, was received.

9 Oct 1790 - John Munro opened the meeting.

13 March 1791 - Patience Brumfield (wife of David Brumfield), and Amelia Smith (wife or widow of John Smith) baptized.

2nd Sabbath in May 1791 - James Johnston and Josiah Oburn, ministering brethren.

Saturday before 3rd Sabbath in June 1791 - Brother Johnston
apply'd for transient membership (not having been dismissed from
Buchmarsh Church. Easter Henton, widow of John Henton,
presented a letter of dismission dated 23 Nov 1766 from Church of
Christ, Cumry Township in Berks Co., Pennsylvania. Amelia
Bowen, wife of Francis Bowen, presented a letter of dismission from
the United Baptist Church of Christ at Mill Creek, Shenandoah Co.,
Virginia, 28 May 1791.

2nd Sabbath in July 1791 - Dinah Talman, wife of Benjamin, and
Elener Gum, widow of Norton Gum, baptized.

13 Aug 1791 - James Riggs, member of a sister church, invited to sit
with us.

10 Sep 1791 - Brother Johnston presented a letter of dismission
from Buckmarsh Church dated last May.

8 Oct 1791 - John Monroe came up and met with us. Ordained
James Johnston.

12 Nov 1791 - Elener Gum was basely begotten with child and
confessed to the fact. Excommunicated. James Riggs presented
letter of dismission from a church on the waters of Peters Creek,
dated 11 Nov 1788. The case of black members or slaves; it was
considered whether they should be admitted to a seat among us on
days of business - resolved that they should. Resolved that John
Stevenson be considered member in full fellowship.

13 Nov 1791 - Baptized Francis Bowen.

4 March 1792 - Mary Webb baptized.

13 May 1792 - Benjamin Talman baptized.

12 Aug 1792 - Ruth Brigs baptized.

8 Dec 1792 - Margaret Harrison to be met with for non-attendance

and also Brother Bowen and wife for same; and Brother Thomas for same.

12 Jan 1793 - Absalom Graves presented a letter of dismission from the Church of Christ on Rapidan River in Culpeper Co.

9 Feb 1793 - The reception of Rozannah Garretson, wife of John Garretson, member of Mill Creek Church, recieved by letter of dismission from said church, is postponed. The advisability of receiving old Brother William Davis was considered.

2nd Sabbath in March 1793 - Lucinda Rice, wife of Jno. Rice, received by letter of dismission from Crooked Run Church in Culpeper Co.

Saturday, June 1793 - Jonathan Latham and Kisandren his wife were received by leter of dismission from Church of Christ of Chopanamsick in Stafford Co. A letter of dismission to be written for Grace Fine who was removed some years past.

10 Aug [1793] - Mr. Hopkins' Doll [probably his slave] again related experience, but was not received.

7 Sep 1793 - Letters of dismission delivered for Sisters Webb and Smith; also a recommendation for Amelia Smith was delivered.

12 Oct [1793] - Mary Woods, formerly Mary Cox, was conversed with about joining this church. She will obtain a new letter of dismission form Ragged Mountain Church, Culpeper County; she had lost her old letter.

7 Dec 1793 - To write for letter of dismission for Absalom Graves and wife. Phebe Harrison (of Smiths Creek) died at age 108. Funeral held on 8 Dec 1793.

10 May 1794 - Mr. Moor's Joe was laid under the censure of the church for, according to Margaret Harrison, propogating a scandelous report as a truth against a member of Sister Harrison's family.

11 May 1794 - Baptized Absalom Lyn and Jenny his wife.

8 June 1794 - Brother Latham's mulatto woman Sucky baptized.

26 July 1794 - Brother Joe was heard after being suspended; it was voted that Sister Margaret Harrison be suspended as well.

9 Aug 1794 - Brother Latham having called upon Margaret Harrison to settle grievances reported that she forgave Mr. Morr's Joe and it was agreed that Joe keep his place in the Church as well as herself, on condition that Joe not have the priviledge of her wench Dine as his wife. Both were restored to the Church.

13 Sep 1794 - Received Margaret Briton into the transient Communion of the Church, she being a member of Buckmarsh Church. Jno. Thomas was granted a letter of dismission.

11 Oct 1794 - Br. Johnston was granted a letter of dismission. Ruth Brig was granted a letter of dismission.

11 April 1795 - Names on contribution list: Bro. Talman and wife, Bro. Lincoln and wife, Bro. Latham and wife, Bro. Bowen and wife, Bro. Lyn and wife, Bro. McFarland and wife, Hannah Harrison, Margret Harrison, M. Thomas, E. Henton, Br. Lockard, Sister Brumfield, --- Briton.

12 March 1796 - Brother Latham requested a letter of dismission for his mulatto woman Sucky - granted. Letters of dismission were granted to Brother Latham and wife and Brother Lyn and wife.

8 Oct 1796 - James Ireland visited and preached. Rhoda Jeffreys, wife of --- Jeffreys, member of Baptist Church of Christ on Lost River, received.

8 Dec 1798 - Thomas Yates gave a letter of dismission from F. T. Church.

Extracts from the minutes of
SMITH'S CREEK BAPTIST CHURCH

This church was constituted in 1774. The minutes begin on 2 Jan 1779. Most of the meetings were held at New Market in Shenandoah County.

Jan 1779 - Christian Cauts was excommunicated for the sin of fornication. Bro. Daniel Mauke was brought before the church for fornication and was laid over till the next monthly meeting [excommunicated]. Sister Elisabeth Couts was brought before the church for profainly swearing and keeping bad company - excommunicated. Sister Catharine Rader was censured for fornication.

Saturday in Feb 1779 - Rudalph Mauke chosen for ordination [as deacon?]. John Runyon chosed for a deacon.

7 Oct 1780 - Nancey Rader was excommunicated for folley. Aaron Solomon offered his experience and was received. Ann Clerck was received by experience.

4 Aug 1781 - William Leach and Sister Margerate Markes was excommunicated for the sin of adultery, "conextion in the same crime."

1st Saturday Nov 1781 - John Laman complained of Sister Ann Clerck and she failing to appear.

1782 March Bro. Mauke complained of Sister Elesabeth Whitman's disorderly way of living. Sara Kersner received.

6 April 1782 - Elesabeth Whitman excommunicated. John Laman and wife dismissed by letter.

3 Aug 1782 - Catharine Auzamus dismissed; also Sarah Kersner, by letter.

7 June 1783 - George Grabiel excommunicated for sin of fornication.

1 Oct 1785 - Lydia McGlamry dismissed.

1st Saturday in Aug 1787 - Rudolph Mauke and Catharine his wife dismissed by letter; also his dau. Barbara dismissed. sister Phebe Flecher received by letter.

3 Nov 1787 - Frederick Whitman received.

1 Dec 1787 - Sary Brannam received.

1st Saturday in Sep 1787 - Experience of Sary Brannam was received.

2 Feb 1788 - Grievance against Peter Good by Abraham Derst and John Neff for the sin of profainly swearing. John Stighler received.

May 1788 - Delinquents: William Davis, Mathias Beaver, Elesabeth Repp, Catharine Huling. John Stighler refused to be baptized.

5 July 1788 - Elesabeth Larkin (?) received.

2 Aug 1788 - Solomon Castner received.

1 Nov 1788 - Charity Woolf received.

7 Feb 1789 - Catharine Hulings asked to answer for her neglecting to attend meetings. She expressed a regard to make it known she was no longer a member of the Methodist Society. Nancey Gordon "gave herself a member."

2 May 1789 - Bettey Harkins excommunicated.

4 July 1789 - Complaint against Dinah Woods for saying things one time and denying it.

5 Sep 1789 - Complaint against Miama Dis and Asa Wayin, a slave of Elasabath Russell; she was excommunicated for the sin of fornication.

24 Oct 1789 - Elizabeth Pitner received.

14 Oct 1789 - Money paid: Anthony Reader £0.15.0; George Rader
£0.15.0; Aron Soloman £0.6.0; John Runyon £0.15.0; Josiah Ozburn
(in clothing) 0.9.0; Ezekiel Herrison ?; John Fifer £0.8.0. Inquiry to
be made as to the reason of Abraham Dirst not attending meetings.

6 March 1790 - Peter Good was visited regarding his not attending
church meetings. Mathias Beaver was visited to find that his family
is in great distance and thus he could not attend.

3 April 1790 - Ezekiel Harrison to obtain a sufficient lease from
Edwin Young for the meeting house. To cite Sarah Branham to
attend the next meeting.

1 May 1790 - John Linan and Sarah Koontz present to take a seat
with us. Peter Good was asked to give his reasons for his absenting
meetings [he gave reason of bad health].

5 June 1790 - Sister Nancy Rite to have a word of reproof.

2 Oct 1790 - John Phifer(?) and wife dismissed by letter.

1 Jan 1791 - The case of William Davis was reconsidered. To enquire
into Peter Good's absences.

5 Feb 1791 - Ezl. Harrison, Walter Newman and Henry Bowen to
consult Mr. Sauge(?) regarding the title to ground for a meeting
house.

5 March 1791 - Sary Coons was invited to set with us.

2 April 1791 - Charles Gordan acknowledged his transgression. The
church has discharged the debt concerning Wm. Davis clothing.

4 June 1791 - To visit Chatrin Ranshaw regarding her not attending
meetings.

2 July 1791 - A distress being brought into the church by Bro.
George Koonts and for Sally Koonts that Ann Wright
[excommunicated] hast been guilty of being catched in bed with a
man several times, also denying the truth at different times. To ask
her to attend the next meeting.

1 Oct 1791 - Letter of dismission to Greenbriar to Sister Pope.

7 Jan 1792 - Charles Gorden gave satisfaction.

3 March 1792 - In the case of Sally Branham she promises to give satisfaction. [Later she did.]

5 May 1792 - Sally Coons was invited to set with us.

28 June 1792 - Relief to be given to Sister Collins.

28 July 1792 - The case of Lewis Blesing for the sin of fornication was reviewed. Henry Hawser and Walter Newman to provide 800 feet each of plank for the next meeting house.

1 Sep 1792 - Nancy Hall as dismist by letter.

6 Oct 1792 - Dismissed Elisabeth Pope by letter.

5 Jan 1793 - Anthony Rader informed the Church that Nancy Gordon had grieved him by joining the Methodists Society. [She later gave full satisfaction.] Charles Gordin's conduct was questioned.

1 June 1793 - Sarah Vinson came forward with a letter of dismission from Upper South River Church; received.

5 April 1794 - Elesabeth Pitner excommunicated. Letter of dismission granted to Anthony Reader and his wife Cathrin.

3 May 1794 - Mary Bligh was received.

6 Sep 1794 - Mrs. Sugdon being present complained that Solomon Cowner behaved ill, speaking falsitites.

1 Dec 1794 - Sister Fletcher requested a letter of dismission.

6 Dec 1794 - George Counar informed of Solomon Castner [Keshner] speaking falsities.

3 April 1796 - Matthias Bever [gave satisfaction at the next meeting], Philip Wolf and Aron Solomon have frequently neglected attending meeetings.

30 April 1796 - William Brim was invited to set with us.

5 Aug 1797 - Samuel Odel took a seat with us.

6 April 1798 - Abraham Darste and wife were granted a letter of dismission.

5 May 1798 - Margret Briten was received into fellowship, she being regularly dismissed from a church of the same faith.

1 Sep 1798 - Application was made by Anderson Moffette for letters of dismission for his brother Walter Moffett and wife; granted. A letter of dismission was granted to Sister Ann Braneman.

2 Aug 1800 - Samuel Cramer took a seat with us.

MARRIAGES BY REV. JOHN ALDERSON, JR.

Following are the records of Rev. John Alderson, Jr. at Linville's Creek, now in Rockingham County and Greenbrier County (now West Virginia). These entries were based on articles appearing in the William and Mary Quarterly, Virginia Valley Records and a photostat copy at the Virginia State Library. It will be seen that major differences appear in the earliest portion of the records. At the time these articles were written the original was held by the Virginia Baptist Historical Society at the University of Richmond. The sources are identified as follows:

[1] William and Mary Quarterly, 2d ser. 8 (1928): 194-202.
[2] Virginia Valley Records, by John W. Wayland, (1930): 153-163.
[3] My interpretation of the photostat and annotations made on the photostat.

Auga. County.
Jenewry 4, 1776. James (Sconee?)[1] or (Sconce)[2] or (Boyd?)[3] with Elizabeth Miller, and William ⋯ with Catherian ⋯[1, 2] or Katherine West [3]

Phillip Custer [1, 2] or Cuper [3] with Elisabeth ⋯ (Levi?) [1, 2] or Wood [3] and Peter Tho⋯ or Sho [1, 2, 3] with Elizbaeth Lee [1, 2] or See [3]

Dunmore County
February 13, 1776. Henry ⋯ [1, 2] or Litos(?)[3] with Rebaca Harden

Auga. County
March ⋯ Holten Muncey(?) and ⋯

April 1, 1776. George Reuble with Catherine ⋯ [1, 2] or West [3]
April 2, 1776. Adam Rader with Clare Ruddel
April 22, 1776. Michal Lime [1, 2] or Laine [3] with Magdalan Harter [1, 2] or Harper(?)[3]
April 23, 1776. Joseph Rambo with Sarah Warren and Evin Phillips with Elisabeth Dever
May 16 1776. ⋯ Dorman and ⋯; May ⋯ King and ⋯; May 23, Nathan Wiatt and Sarah Smith; Mary 23, James Hall and Ann

Cristy.

May 21, 1776. William Tyrie with Elisabeth Prise, both of Dunmore.
May 23, 1776. Nathan Wiatt with Sarah Smith, Dunmore
May 23, 1776. James Hall with Ann Cristy
On the day of setlement with the Curiot was June 4 1776
David Rader with Ruth Henton [1, 2] or Kenton [3].
June 25, 1776. James Prise with Catherian Smith
July 26, 1776. Joseph Rodgers with Catherine Funk
August 13, 1776. Jacob Teganfus [1, 2] or Zeganfus [3] with
    Christenah Brilian [1, 2] or Britian [3]
Sept 17, 1776. Jacob Cortne with Catherian Panter
November 13(?) 1776, Bennedick Alsie(?) [1, 2] or Atsee (Alfee?) [3]
    with Elisabeth Williams from Dunmore
January 16, 1777. John Jackman with Hannah George
Januarwary 28, 1777. John Mitchel with Annmary Jacobin.
Febuary 3, 1777. Jacob Vendevorter [1] or Vendwarter
    (Vendeverter) [2, 3] with Elisabeth Bibl(?) [1, 2] or Bilel(?) [3]
Iasaac Strickler with Susanah Blubaker February 21, 1777
March 3, 1777. Blank
March 22, 1777. William Evens with Mary Fleming.
Ap[rial 15, 1777. William Vance with Barbery Crider.
Aprial 28, 1777. Daniel Branerman with Mary Durst
May 12, 1777. Peter Perselul with Marget Selsar(?)
May 19, 1777. Barefoot Runyan with Margret Rambo
Edward Millon with Mary White August 11, 1777
August 17, 1777. James Jamason with Martha Crow [2, 3] or Crew
    [1]
Carlile Hanes with Hannah Waring August 18, 1777
Greenbryer October 21, 1777 John Petty with Margreat Hundly [1,
    2] or Handly [3]
Decembr. 25 1777 George Lee [1, 2] or See [3] with Martha George.
Febry 10, 1778. Elexander Hoseck with Sarah Tolle
Febry 23, 1778. Wm. McGuire with Mary Shirley
March 19, 1778. Dennis Neel with Ann Ibbet
Aprial 2, 1778. Robart Raburn with Sarah McGuire
April 10, 1778. Wm. Loctridge with Sarah Linsy
April 30, 1778. John Woods with Abigal Estel.
May 4, 1778. William Hogan with Sarah Sullavan
June 1, 1778. John Baughman with Catherian Shirley

June 21, 1778. David Kuke with Sarah (Pullin?[1, 2] or Dullin [3]
July 14, 1778. Oziah Barns with Jane Flemings
August 7, 1778. John Ewins with Easther Cook
June 4, Received from John Alderson three pounds five shillings
   being the amount of ten marriage fees. Alexr. Balmain Clk.
   curate of Augusta Parish.
December 23, 177-. Walis Estel with Jane Wright
January 4, 1779. Jessie Jarratt with Sarah Cambel
January 18, 1779. David Rees [1, 2] or Rahl(?) [3] with Grisile Lagua
January 19, 1779. John McCalester with Anna Loagua
January 28, 1779. David Rodgers with Elisabeth Palintine
Febry 2, 1779. George Clandennan with Jamminah McNeel
Febry 21, 1779. Abraham Baker and Sarah Smith
March 5, 1779. John Sopes [1, 2] or Sorres [3] with Margrat Miller
March 12, 1779. John Clarke with Elisabeth Cortner
June 8, 1779. John Gilkason with Nansy Davis
June 7, 1779. Jacob Chapman with Margrat Burns
June 22, 1779. John Dankadys [1, 2] or Dauhady [3] with
   Rhobackah Lewis
July 19, 1779. John McGuier with Elisabeth Gottel [1] or Cottel(?)[2,
   3]
Patrick Murphy with Elisabeth Spenser [1, 2] or Swenser [3]
August 21, 1779. Charles Smith with Elisabeth Rosety
August 24, 1779. Jacob Man with Mary Kisaner [1, 2] or Kesines [3]
September 5, 1779. John Oncel Blare with Esther Davis
September 16, 1779. Joseph Riffe with Margrat Carpenter
October 8, 1779. Samuel Clark with Margaret Burgan
Edward Barrat with Sussan Griff
November 8, 1779. James M--- [1, 2] or Meek [3] with Sarah
   Gilkason
James M---[1] or --- [2] or Bryan [3] with Sarah Nash November ---
   1779
--- Perrigen [1, 2] or R--- Perriger(?) [3] with Susanah Burgan
   December 20, 1779
January 5, 1780. Jacob Price with Wereford Hillary [1] or Weneford
   Tillary [3]
January 10, 1780. James Kitchans with Jane Pattason
February 14, 1780. Danial McMullan [1, 2] or McMuttan [3] with
   Nelly Keenany
March 1, 1780. Thomas Spenser with Mary Evison

March 3, 1780. Phillip Haman with Christen Kuke
March 20, 1780. Valantine Smathers with Barbery Wimer
Aprial 18, 1780. Oen Jarrot with Mary Doran
April 19, 1780. Thomas Shelten with Elisabeth Cavender
James Williams with Sibna Wilson May 9, 1780
May 11, 1780. John Wallis with Jane Miller
May 2, 1780. John McMullan with Fransinah Gully
June 13, 1780. William Hunter Cavindish with Jane Murphy
June 15, 1780. Wm. Dun with Hannah Welch
Do Richard Homes with Martha Hearod.
July 5, 1780. James Christy with Sarrah Scarbrough
July 7, 1780. Samuel Jamison with Rhobacah Ward
July 13, 1780. George Frazer with Rosana Reyley
July 21, 1780. John Crane with Easther Kirk
August 23, 1780. James Howard with Hannah Geffers
September --1780. John Lee [1, 2] or See [3] with Margrat Gurrat
September 28, 1780. Henery Davis with Martha Crage
October 10, 1780. Mathew Creed with Elisabeth Carlile
October 12, 1780. Cornelius Miller with Ann James
October 19, 1780. Richard McCalester with Margrat Nicholus
October 19, 1780. Henery Howard with Isbill Griffin
October 19, 1780. Thomas Bird with Margrat Tolbart
November 20, 1780. William Cooper with Fanny Esthel [1, 2] or
    Eathol(?)[3]

Wm. Mary Ellit with Elizabeth Philson. December 5, 1780
Do Simon Acers with Mary Smith
December 12, 1780. Thomas Cuper with Ann Roack [1, 2] or Roach
    [3]
December 22, 1780. William Shanks with Sarah Hanby [1, 2] or
    Hanley [3]
December 26, 1780. Robert Boid [1, 2] or Baid [3] with Mary Glass
Do. Wm. Oharra with Margrat Tincher [1, 2] or Tinsher[3]
Jenuary 2, 1781. Gordan Griffin with Catharian Kichener [1, 2] or
    Kishener [3]
Jenuary 11, 1781. Michel Keeney with Catharian Lewis
Janury 30, 1781. Brice Miller with Elisabeth Bradshaw
Febry 6, 1781. James McNut [1, 2] or McNeel [3] with Sidny Evens
    [1, 2] or Ewens [3]
Do. Littelton West with Eliner Gallaway

Febry 17, 1781. Wm. Jeffers with Susanah Johnson
Do Joseph West with Agness Carpenter
February 18, 1781. James Williams with Catheren Nicholus
Febry 25, 1781. Antony Sebrok [1, 2] or Schoh [3] with Nansy
    Truckwell [1] or Tuckwell [2, 3]
March 1, 1781
David Cutlip with Jane Burris [1, 2] or Burns [3]
April 9, 1781. David Jamison with Hannah Rickerds [1, 3] or
    Richards [2]
April 12, 1781. Richard Wilson with Mary Rogers
June 4, 1781 [2] or June 11, 1781 ⋯ [1, 2] or John [3] Hutcheson
    with Rhobaka Hutcheson
June 11 John Davis with Elizabeth McFarlen
June 14, 1781. George Alderson with Sarah Osburn
⋯ John Fenton with Mary Ann Fairs(?)
June 15, 1781. Daniel McDowel with Euphamia Huston
July 2, 1781. Thomas Cooper with Margrat Hilyard
August 28, 1781. David Trimble with Lusey Lasy. [Lacy - 2]
October 5, 1781. Wm. Harris with Sarah Persival
October 10, 1781. Edward Moss with Barbery Boyer
October 29, 1781. Edward Pemberton with Mary Anderson
October 29, 1781. John Kirny [1, 2] or King (Keany?) [3] with Mary
    Samson
November 23, 1781. John Clapole with Rhobecah Osburn
November 27, 1781. Moses Turpen with Magdilia Black
November 29, 1781. Wm. Comer with Mary McCarty
December 19, 1781. Joseph Edwards with Agniss Ramsy
December 24, 1781. Charles Hines [1, 2] or Higes(?) [3] with Marget
    Dickson
January 9, 1782. Charles Wimer with Lettis Hannah
January 23, 1782. John Russel with Susanah Day
    William Gilliner with Hannah Aclen [1, 2] or Acten [3]. By
    license.
January 30, 1782. Edward Barret with Easter Burnside
February 5 1782. James Oharra with Elisabeth Davis
February 9 [1, 2], or 7 [3], James Kelly with Agness Caperton [1, 2]
    or Cawerton [3]
February 11, 1782. John Cincaid with Elisabeth Gilaspy
March 3, 1782. ⋯ Miller ⋯. [1]
March 3, 1782. Richard and Mille.[2]

March 19, 1782. Walter Davis with Ellener Herbert
April 5, 1782. Robard Bogs with Sarah Fluston [1, 2] or Huston [3]
April 5 Joseph Hanes with Barbery Rife
16 James Knox with Margret Johnson
25 Peter Woods with Jael Kavanaugh
April 29 [1, 2] or April 27 [3] Angel Conner with Matte Flemmen
May 1, 1782. James Hoogens with Jane Cook
May 9, 1782. Iasaac Anglin [1, 2] or Auglin [3] with Nancy Dier
May 15, 1782. John Snotgrass with Ilny [1] or Elny [2] Murphy
May 23, 1782. David Mordah (Murdock?) with Marget Jemson [1] or
    Tomson [2]
May 28, 1782. Robart Nicol with Margat Gray
July 14, 1782. Timothy Sweet with Catorin Nurss [1] or Nurf [2]
July 15, 1782. James Stiles with Jane Harwood
July 23, 1782. Wm. Doderidge with Rhebecah Doharty.
July 30, 1782. James Sconce with Lidea Britton
August 9, 1782. William Sconce with Margrat Murley
August 13, 1782. John Shoumaker with Elisabeth Youlekem
August 22, 1782. Wm. Toney with Leah Gatlift
----. Thomas Fulton and Susannah Kisenyer. [2, 3]
August 22, 1782. Samuel Estell with Jane Tase
September 1, 1782. Benjamin Johnston with Lidea Ford
September 1, 1782. George Owens and Mary Cotton
September 14, 1782. George Stuart with Christin Holshople
September 17, 1782. Isaac Fisher with Rachel Riggs
Sepr 19, 1782. Isaac Poulton with Ann Green
September 26, 1782. Samuel Black with Mary Donaly
October 22, 1782. Wm. Baly with Jane Johnson
October 29, 1782. Richard Mullen with Elisabeth Lewis
October 31, 1782. James Harris with Mary Edwards
14 November. John Erwin with Jane King
18 November. John Frier with Elisabeth Biggs
20 November. George Dickson with Verona Venbebber
Novr. 26, 1782. John Curry with Isblla Ellison
December 17, 1782. Ase Ellison with Elisabeth Kilpatrick
December 20, 1782. George Stevenson with Elener Clendenen
9 Jnery 1783. Robart Johnson with Martha Raulston
30 Jnry 1783. John Gibson with Sarah Stevenson
10 Febry 1783. John Dunbar with Elisabeth Osbun
11 Febry 1783. Iasaac Burgan with Mary Tacket

25 Febry 1783. William Maddry with Elisabeth Man
June 18, 1783. William Hicks with Hannah Garrad
July 29, 1783. Jacob Kissinger with Sarah Fulton
September 9, 1783. James Walker with Catherian Miller
September 9, 1783. James Gilkason with Elisabeth Currens
September 22, 1783. Charles Friend and Rachel Tacket
Sept. 30, 1783. David Lodinback with Kezia Ward
October 20, 1783. Ralph Gyates with Jennet Wiley
[Source 2 also suggests the possibility: Ralph G. Yates and Jennet
    Wiley]
November 27, 1783. Joseph Williams with Elisabeth Raulston [1, 2]
    or Ralston [3]
December 9, 1783. Adam Man with Mary Maddy.
December 9, 1783. Garrat McCallester with Susannah Crage.
December 9, 1783. Abraham Dewit with Catherin Baras [1] or Barns
    [2]
27 December 1783. Abraham Neetal [1] or Noetel [2] or Nettel [3]
    with Mary McDannal
22 Jany 1784. Elexander Reed with Rhebecah Mitchel
May 6, 1784. William Booten with Matilda Sturgess [1, 2] or Sturgis
    [3]
May 13, 1784. John Carlile with Rosanah Souards
May 24, 1784. William Wiley with Karanhapouch Catliff [1] or
    Gatliff [2]
June 19, 1784. William Cansfax [1] with Elisabeth Miller
June 19, 1784. Joshua Townsen with Elisabeth Caperton
Sept. 6, 1784. William Adams with Sarah Sturdg [1] or Sturde [2]
Sept. 14, 1784. Thomas Wyate with Rachel Burnside.
September 21, 1784. Danial Nicholus with Rhebecah Sturde
November 9, 1784. Luke West with Rosey Acars.
December 6, 1784. William Haze with Levine Gully.
7 December 1784. Willis Morris with Elisabeth Garrat
14 December 1784. Joseph Hickenbottom with Mary Reed
December 16, 1784. James Steephens with Mary Man.
30 December 1784. Ambrus Jones with Martha Crage
Jenury 17, 1785. William Butcher with Margarat Donnaly
18 Jenury 1785. Andrew Cissiner with Saveney Nester
19 Jenury 1785. Edward Price with Elisabeth Newhouse
Jnry 25, 1785. Mitchel Porter with Penelope West
Febry 8, 1785. George Parker with Anny Maddy

Febry 8, 1785. Paul Long with Elisabeth Maddy
Febry 8, 1785. Thomas Nickell with Jeane [1] Joane [2] Reiburn
March 8, 1785. Martin Turpen with Nancy Fleming
March 8, 1785. Jeremiah Carpenter with Elisabeth Hamm
March 8, 1785. Mosely Childris with Elisabeth Jeffries
Aprial 7, 1785. Robart Ervin with Barbara Nicol
Aprial 18, 1785. Robart Johnston with Catherian Doren
Aprial 24, 1785. David Garrat with Susanah Hicks
May 24, 1785. John Lewis, Jr., with Rachel Viney
June 8, 1785. Samuel Dunbar with Debrough George
June 21, 1785. Samual Kincaide with Mary Tincher
June 29, 1785. Peter Venbebber with Eleaner Venbebber
July 1, 1785. James Bales with Rebecaha Bracken
July 3, 1785. Math Forbs with Easther McMullon
July 6, 1785. John Keppers with Rebecah Patterson
July 8, 1785. Simon Cooper with Margret Tincher
July 22, 1785. Peter Venbebber with Sarah Yolkecome
August 8, 1785. John Maddy with Barbery Miller
September 21, 1785. James Shannaday with Jane Williams
September 21, 1785. Heugh [1] or Hough [2} Caperton with
    Rhodeiea Sturgen
October 13, 1785. John Curry with Mary Johnston
November, --, 1785. James Fleming with Mary Kinder
Novr 5, 1785. Thomas Trimble with Abigal Gatliff
November 10, 1785. Joseph Miller with Marget Best
November 21, 1785. Mark Lacey with Agness McDonald
December 14, 1785. William Sprowl with Jane Hamelton
December 29, 1785. Levi Low with Sarah Kincaed
Janewary 10, 1786. James Bailey with Nancy Tharp
Febry 14, 1786. John Scaggs with Kitty Hicks
Febry 21, 1786. James Wilson with Loucresta Sturgen
Febry 21, 1786. Henry Green with Sarah Henderson
Febry 21, 1786. William Jones with Sarah Reburn
March 2, 1786. William Carteren with Jane Miller
March 2, 1786. William Holly with Prudence Castile
March 9, 1786. Richard Hicks with Jane Skags
May 3, 1786. David Scarbrouh with Elisabeth Anderson
May 6, 1786. Thomas Williams with Elisabeth Nickolus
June 18, 1786. Aaron Turpen with Jane Barns
July 3, 1786. William Lacey with Martha Blankenship

October 3, 1786. George Doughaty with Juda Holshopel
6 October 1786. Thomas Spencer with Elisabeth Perkins
6 October 1786. James Hayns with Ann Ellison
10 October 1786. Samuel Peepels with Sarah Tincker
17 October 1786. Travis Booten with Ruth Estele
17 October 1786. John Canterbery with Nancy Lowe
November 30, 1786. Simon Shramm with Barbary Belew
December 18, 1786. George Lewis with Leah Viney
Jenewary 23, 1787. Obadiah Hammonds with Elisabeth Skaggs
30 Jenewaray 1787. Joseph Sawyers with Elisabeth McDad [1] or
    McDade [2, 3]
March 8, 1787. William Johnston with Elisabeth Hicks
15 March 1787. Nimrod Tackete with Anne Howard
Aprial 17, 1787. David Miller with Ruth Burditt
19 Aprial 1787. William Trimbel with Mary Fleming
30 Aprial 1787. Iasaac Paul with Massy Eleson
May 7, 1787. Ezekiel Parsons with Elisabeth Kesener
July 3, 1787. Wm. Daghaty with Lidia Tacket
September 3, 1787. Hugh Paul with Ann Killpatrick
13 September 1787. Wm. Drawdy with Ruth Ellison
19 September 1787. Griffith Garton with Hannah Miller
25 September 1787. Peter Dick with Barbara Null
October 30, 1787. John Fauster with Clairy Burdit
November 5, 1787. John Ellis with Anne Paul
8 November 1787. Alexander Wilson - Mary Dickson
15 November 1787. John Hansford - Jean Morris
25 November 1787. John Claston - Bridgit Martin or Williams
26 November 1787. William Slavin - Nancy Ingram
Febry 9, 1788. Samual Ramsy - Elisabeth Griffith
28 Febry 1788. Robart Tincher with Nancy Dickson
March 18, 1788. Solomon Turpin - Mary West
Aprial 24, 1788. David Keeny - Peninah Bails
May 1, 1788. John Peck Forde - Jane Frogg
15 May 1788. Henery McDannel - Hannah Bryan
22 May 1788. Levi Morris - Magrat Garrot
June 26, 1788. John Lacy - Sarah Porter
June 30, 1788. Abraham Henderson - Ann Blanton
July 5, 1788. Edward Goand - Nelly Needham

19 July 1788. Peter Likins with Mary Garrat
Sept. 15, 1788. Davis Alderson and Leah Carrol
Novmr. 10, 1788. James Claypole and Elener Butler
Novmr. 12, 1788. Benjamin Morris and Nancy Garrat
March 25, 1790. Wm. Dickens and Feaby Lewis
Aprial 2, 1790. Danial Javen and Martha Thompson
Aprial 29, 1790. Moses Wilson and Martha Rickey
May 3, 1790. Adam Man and Polly Flinn
May 30, 1790. Danial Jones and Isbel Hunter
August 9, 1790. Jeremiah Roach and Elisabeth Null
Sept. 1, 1790. Nicholus Null and Ruth Ellis
Oct. 24, 1790. William Griffits and Mary Lewis
Oct. 26, 1790. Cothel Lively and Sally Moddy [1] or Meddy [2]
November 1, 1790. Nathan Robinet and Sarah Burnsides
November 4, 1790. Robart Hews and Elisabeth Tincher
November 8, 1790. James Smith and Sarah Piper
November 22, 1790. George Hews and Margrat Johnstun [1] or
    Johnston [2]
November 25, 1790. John Humphries and Jane Ward
December 11, 1790. Joseph Black and Esther Dison
December 13, 1790. William Cook and Jane Young
December 23, 1790. William McGinstery and Elisabeth Hail
December 23, 1790. Robart Renick and Polly Hamilton
December 28, 1790. Henry Hedrick and Betsy Comber
Janry 10, 1791. Ezkel Mathews and Jane McSparrin
Jnry 11, 1791. John Williams and Martha McMillen
Janry 13, 1791. Adam Eyhole and Mary Britan
Jnry 18, 1791. Hugh Williams and Jane Bell
Jnry 27, 1791. Edward Farlo and Lettece McM---
Jnry 31, 1791. John Paterson and Elisabeth Mullin
Feby 7, 1791. Ezkial Jenkins and Anna Ford
Feby 24, 1791. Michel Miller and Elisabeth Smith
Feby 24, 1791. Andrew Wilson and Janey Hutchison
March 2, 1791. Duncen [1] or Duncan [2] Graham and Anna Parsons
March 3, 1791. Grigsby Foster and Martha Handly
March 5, 1791. Andrew Boggs and Susanah Bowen
March 6, 1791. Aron Ewing and Elionere Bartley
March 6, 1791. Robart Harvie and Esther Bartley
March 6, 1791. Griffith Evins and Martha McNiel
March 8, 1791. John Lowance and Sarah Holly

March 8, 1791. Patrick Murpha [1] Murphy [2] and Ann Miller
Aprial 29, 1791. John Lewis and Rhebecah Sowards
June 28, 1791. Louther Smith and Barbery Loudeback
August 1, 1791. Robart Louis and Betsy Morris
August 4, 1791. Francies Watkins and Anna Donnaly, Kanhawy [1]
   or Kanawha [2] County.
August 12, 1791. Aron Newman and Catharine Blair
Sept. 9, 1791. James Kennaday and Rachel Scarbrough
Sept. 13, 1791. Joseph Dicson and Nancy McClung
Sept. 16, 1791. Jacob Fodge and Christina Barcks
Sept. 27, 1791. Andee Showens and Betsy McGuire
Oct. 24, 1791. William Kindir and Talitha West
November 22, 1791. Thomas Kincaid - Hannah Vine (Viney?)
December 1, 1791. Boyd Miller and Mary Story
December 1, 1791. Thomas Masterson and Jane McClung
17 December 1791. James Cash and Pheby Lacy
January 19, 1791. David Jacocke and Lilly Smith
Febry 7, 1792. Thomas George and Catren McCoy
Febry 15, 1791. Rubin Bootan and Mary Dick
Aprial 17, 1792. Ephram Claypole and Lucy Arbough
May 31, 1792. Thomas Holaday and Elisabeth Ballentine
This is to certify to home it May Concern that we the subcribers
   have reason to believe from all Sirccustances that James Parsons
   is Ded. Givin under our hands this 3 Day of March 1791. Richard
   George, Robert Reed, Alexander Hosick, Benjamen Reed, James
   Chambers, Angel Connel, Jacob Kilyon.
Sept. 11, 1794. Elexander Porter and Mary Mathews
Oct. 2, 1794. John Patterson and Betsy Carroway
Novr. 12, 1794. Elija Cornwell and Ruth Swobe
Novr. 20, 1794. Robart McDowel and Mary Harbert
Novr. 27, 1794. Bedford Fenter [1] or Foster [2] and Lissy Cornwell
Novr. 27, 1794. Natis [1] or Hatis [2] Legg and Elizabeth Cornwell
Decemr. 9, 1794. Joseph Phillips and Pheybe Thomas
Decemr. 11, 1794. John Hinchman and Sarah Vincen [1] or Vincon
   [2]
Janry. 1, 1795. Wm. Legg and Susanah Vincen [1] or Vincon [2]
Janry. 1, 1795. James Fauster and Elisabeth Humphrees
Janry. 6, 1795. Mathew Leech and Polly Gullett
Janry. 22, 1795. John Jordan and Cath. Blare
Janry. 22, 1795. John Lewis and Elizabeth Edwards

Janry. 22, 1795. Moses Shepherd and Mary Holly
Janry. 29, 1795. Moses Massy and Rebecha Lewis
Janry. 29, 1795. Adam Fifer and Cathrine Myers.
Janry. 30, 1795. Jacob Althair and Susanah Fleshman.
Febry. 12, 1795. Wm. Taylor and City Alsup.
Febry. 25, 1795. Wm. Carrel and Catharine Shoamaker [1] or
    Shoemaker [2].
March 10, 1795. Henery Carraway and Margrat Smith.
Aprial 19, 1795. John Greves [1] Groves [2] and Catherine Seivers
May 5, 1795. John Morehead and Jane Nicholus
May 7, 1795. Nicholas Kerns and Laney Vanordal
May 7, 1795. Thomas Blare and Nancy Callison
May 12, 1795. Saml. Blare and Peggy Vaugheb
May 21, 1795. William Williams and Mary Watts
June 30, 1795. Charles Arbuckal and Esther Shiles
Sept. 1, 1795. John Levese and Mary Cambel
Sept. 3, 1795. Isaac Garrat and Magt. Macey
Sept. 15, 1795. James McCoy and Betsey Hines
Oct. 20, 1795. Robart Sampels and Maryann Walker
Oct. 20, 1795. Jonathan Mathews and Hannah Macy
November 17, 1795. Jacob Ellis and Margarat Griffith
November 26, 1795. James Griffith and Susannah Davis
Decembr. 29, 1795. Esom Leach and Jane Handly
Decembr. 31, 1795. Enoch Fauster and Margrat Wallis
Jnry. 28, 1796. Isaac Lewis and Helana Blake
March 19, 1791. This day setled with John Flin and Ballance Due to
    him three Gallons and three Quarts Whisky.
Febry. 16, 1796. George Swobe and Nancey Givin
Febry. 16, 1796. Edward McClung and Sarah Vincy [1] Viney [2]
Febry. 25, 1796. John Hanna and Eliz. Smith
March 6, 1796. Cpt. Maddies Nagres
March 10, 1796. Wm. Butler and Tacey Gray
Aprial 19, 1796. Thomas Smithson and Marget Alderson
May 3, 1796. Jesse Carpenter and Jenny Rite
June 7, 1796. Thos. Feamster and Mary McClung
July 12, 1796. William Lewis and Dinah Vincy [1] or Viney [2]
August 9, 1796. Henry Miller and Barbara Arbaugh
August 30, 1796. Joseph McMullen and Jane Arbaugh
Sept. 13, 1796. Henry Newhous and Elizabeth Claypole
Oct. 27, 1796. John Wethers [1] or Withers [2] and Elizabeth Smith

Novmr. 15, 1796. James Phillips and Elizabeth Lewis (?)
November 24, 1796. Joseph Scaggs and Anna Lewis
Feby. 2, 1797. Wm. Wiley and Mary Nicholus
April 5, 1797. John Byrnsides and Elizabeth Alexander
May 13, 1797. John Keen and Noomia [1] or Neomia [2] Keen
August 24, 1797. John Carter and Cathrine Mite [1] or Hite (?) [2]
Sept. 21, 1797. George Nikle and Margeret Neilson
Decembr. 27, 1797. Charles Birdit and Elizabeth Legg
Jnry. 2, 1798. Tolison Shewma... (Shewmate or Shewmaker) and
    Elizabeth Birdit
Jnry. 9, 1798. Samual Ingels and Elizabeth Scaggs
Jnry. 20. John Prichet and Mary Taylor
March 4, 1798. Samual Canterbery and Jane Dicks
May 5, 1798. Edmond Meddows and Sarah Calloway
May 29, 1798. John Perry and Jane Nelson
In the article appearing in William and Mary Quarterly is the
    following:
"Anent the Greenbrier and other West Virginia records, Mr. Henry
W. Scarborough of Philadelphia makes the following observations:
    'The History of Monroe County, West Virginia, shows that
    James Christy, whom the Rev. Mr. Alderson married to
    Sarah Scarbrough on July 5, 1780, was the first pastor of the
    Rehobeth Methodist Church about two miles from Union,
    now Monroe County, West Virginia; and he and his
    brothers-in-law, William Scarbrough and James Scarbrough,
    were among the five trustees, as is shown by said history.
    They were the children of Robert Scarborough, my ancestor,
    mentioned by you in the History of Shenandoah County and
    who settled somewhere on the banks of the North Branch of
    the Shenandoah River, as is shown by a deed on record in
    Philadelphia and by his letter, as being about a mile from
    the Quaker meeting on Holman's Creek and about an equal
    distance from a mill, probably Neff's Mill. I do not believe
    that this marriage record has been published anywhere and
    I would think that even the marriages performed at
    Greenbrier would be of great historical use, because
    probably most of them were persons who had removed from
    the Shenandoah Valley or eastern Virginia.' Date April 26,
    1928."

MARRIAGES IN ROCKINGHAM COUNTY

From John W. Wayland's, Virginia Valley Records, pp. 7-12, taken from records in the county clerk's office at Harrisonburg.

James Boyles and Rosanna Boon, 4 Jan 1795.
Martin Cuntraman and Magaret Stolts, 13 Jan 1795.
James Williamson and Kezia Thomas, 15 Jan 1795.
Jacob Hickam and Catharina Comer, 25 Jan 1795.
John Reagan and Elenor Kyle, 26 Jan 1795.
Frederick Armintrout and Bearbara Monger, 3 Feb 1795.
John Kilburn and Mary Erwin, 24 Feb 1795.
Jacob Miller and Margaret Hemphill, 4 March 1795.
James Boyles and Rosanna Boon, 8 March 1795.
Thomas Hopkins and Sarah Erwin, 10 March 1795.
William Morrison and Margaret Nickoles, 24 March 1795.
Daniel McCartney and Sarah Price, 7 April 1795.
Ezekiel Green and Anne Lokey, 14 April 1795.
James Ervin and Grace Shanklin, 15 Arpil 1795.
Thomas McKinsey and Margaret Thomas, 24 April 1795.
Jacob Cokenhour and Susanna Rader, 26 April 1795.
Henry King and Elizabeth Smith, 27 April 1795.
Robert Shanklin and Margaret Rader, 28 April 1795.
Jacob Marks and Mary Cherryholmes, 2 May 1795.
John Miller and Nancy Wisehart, 25 May 1795.
John Messeck and Sarah Teagy, 5 June 1795.
John Cable and Elizabeth Smith, 8 June 1795.
Charles Chestnut and Elizabeth Robertson, 9 June 1795.
George Bell and Nancy Ervin, 12 June 1795.
James Messeck and Mary Tounsley, 22 June 1795.
Henry Moyers and Sarah Bryant, 22 June 1795.
Dennis O'Bryan and Nancy Green, 22 June 1795.
Archibald Rutherford and Jean Burges, 23 June 1795.
Zachariah Fields and Ann Hamilton, 25 June 1795.
Jacob Passinger and Catharine Cash, 10 July 1795.
John Long and Mary Whitsell, 20 July 1795.
Thomas Brill and Mary Headrick, 3 Aug 1795.
Isaac Hammer and Susanna Bowman, 11 Aug 1795.
Philip Awrey and Elizabeth Circle, 29 Aug 1795.

Michall Joseph and Mary Bowland, 14 Sep 1795.
Abraham Huffman and Dolly Tenkle, 23 Sep 1795.
John Davice and Sarah Ewin, 24 Sep 1795.
Frederick Coniker and Rachel Wiseman, 28 Sep 1795.
Johnston Guinn and Polly Pry, 29 Sep 1795.
Benj. Agle and Mary Boshang, 15 Oct 1795.
James Campbell and Amelia Harrison, 5 Nov 1795.
Williamm Woodford and Hannah Mass, 6 Nov 1795.
Christian Bowars and Elizabeth Andres, 26 Nov 1795.
John Vance and Jane Green, 4 Dec 1795.
Michael Waren and Esther Shanklin, 9 Dec 1795.
John Crotzer and Eleoner Waren, 10 Dec 1795.
John Graham and Sarah Dehart, 24 Dec 1795.
John Caplinger (Keplinger) and Betsy Roler, 29 Dec 1795.
John Hall and Elesebeth Gragg, 2 Jan 1796.
Jacob Cash and Elizabeth Sellers, 5 Jan 1796.
Michael Circle and Rebeca Daugherty, 6 Jan 1796.
John Rader and Susanna Curry, 12 Feb 1796.
Daniel Oliver and Sarah Mole, 27 Feb 1796.
Abram Christman and Polly Johnson, 1 March 1796.
John Christman and Ann Harrison, 10 March 1796.
David Mynes (?) and Elizabeth Kiney, 17 March 1796.
George Berry and Margaret Green, 20 April 1796.
John Bowman and Eve Steet, 25 April 1796.
Archebald Hopkins and Margaret Shanklin, 12 May 1796.
John Book and Barbara Miller, 24 May 1796.
Peter Pasinger and Hannah Snider, 30 May 1796.
Frederick Fickner and Magdalene Earhart, 2 June 1796.
John Layburn and Jane McDowell, 8 June 1796.
Solomon Huffman and Elizabeth Finkle (Tinkle?), 10 June
    1796.
Peter Beard and Mary Eavy, 18 June 1796.
John Mathias and Barbarrey Dispanet, 5 July 1796.
Charls Youst and Polly Brock, 5 July 1796.
John Pitt and Elizabeth Matthews, 22 July 1796.
Benjamin Webb and Sarah Hamilton, 2 Aug 1796.
George Monger and Frances Hestant(?), 2 Aug 1796.
Peter Moore and Sally Sheltman, 24 Aug 1796.
Daniel Finn and Mary Erwin, 8 Sep 1796.
John Herrington and Sally(?) Boshang, 19 Sep 1796.

John Carrell and Deborah Rader, 27 Sep 1796.
Samuel Leaney and Mary Harrison, 28 Sep 1796.
Moses Norman and Mary Higgins, 3 Oct 1796.
John Pence and Mary Ewin, 6 Oct 1796.
Robert Fairbearn and Mary Jackson, 7 Oct 1796.
Christian Sidel and Susanah Bowen, 8 Oct 1796.
Jacob Hoover and Elizabeth Shoemaker, 18 Oct 1796.
George Eary and Mary Cougler, 20 Oct 1796.
Joseph Byerly and Kathren Landis, 8 Nov 1796.
John Twitwiler and Mary Strough, 21 Nov 1796.
Stephen Dorsey and Patience Proctor, 24 Nov 1796.
Elijah Moore and Leday Reeves, 28 Nov 1796.
John Howman and Catherine Simmers, 6 Dec 1796.
Benjamin Groos and Hannah Swagget, 10 Dec 1796.
Jacob Yankey and Mary Shrum, 19 Dec 1796.
Samuel Coffman and Katy Orabough, 20 Dec 1796.
Abraham Pupp and Sevile Miller, 25 Dec 1796.
Augustine Bowman and Rachel Dunlap, 26 Dec 1796.
Casper Pasinger and Eve Snider, 26 Dec 1796.
Robert Jackson and Mary Gum, 26 Dec 1796.
Danel Brunk and Magreat Grace, 1 Jan 1797.
Charles Kyle and Jean Kyle, 6 Jan 1797.
David Farquer and Mary Magaughey, 11 Jan 1797.
William Orabough and Mary Stoutlemire, 21 Jan 1797.
Jacob Trumbo and Polly Hughes, 6 Feb 1797.
Jacob Stoutlemires and Barbara Orabough, 18 Feb 1797.
Gabriel Smith and Susannah Yeates, 27 Feb 1797.
Adam Smelcer and Mary Kretzinger, 28 Feb 1797.
Adam Curry and Phebe Hickman, 13 March 1797.
John Cuntriman and Christena Sitley, 6 April 1797.
George Ryen and Mary Riner, 6 April 1797.
John McCara and Hannah Bell, 16 April 1797.
Michael Pickle and Elizbeth Witzel, 17 April 1797.
John Green and Susanna Winter, 24 April 1797.
Henry Staulp and Catharina Hoe, 24 April 1797.
Michael Crowbarger and Elizbeth Thompson, 29 April 1797.
Peter Hauver and Modalana Aedir, 7 May 1797.
John McNeil and Patience Beard, 10 May 1797.
Samuel Wisemanb and Polly Bowger, 10 May 1797.
Ezekiel Logan and Margaret Harrison, 22 May 1797.

Mathias Moyers and Mary Collens, 23 May 1797.
Christian Kite and Agness Hestant, 6 June 1797.
Jacob Sheets and Mary Martin, 6 June 1797.
Jacob Showalter and Sophia Softly, 24 July 1797.
Martin Nave and Elizabeth Deran, 24 July 1797.
George Crowbarger and Susanna Sipe, 1 Aug 1797.
George Ruebush and Elizabeth Wheelbarger, 1 Aug 1797.
Charles Beggs and Dorotha Trumbo, 1 Aug 1797.
Ferdinand Lair, Preacher
John Bower and Magdelena Andes, 2 Aug 1797.
William Baily and Lucy Croohed, 11 Aug 1797.
John Headrick and Molly Kester, 28 Aug 1797.
Gorden Rogers and Francis Downey, 30 Aug 1797.
Christian Laundis and Madelena Byerly, 2 Sep 1797.
Peter Leonard and Elizabeth Bowers, 9 Sep 1797.
Joseph Showwalter and Lydia Ronk, 12 Sep 1797.
Peter Bish and Phebe Blazea, 12 Sep 1797.
Benjamin Ralston and Margaret Henry, 12 Sep 1797.
John Haney and Margaret Miller, 15 Sep 1797.
George Leonard and Susanna Rodes, 17 Sep 1797.
John Davis and Sarah Dokertey, 19 Sep 1797.
John Keplinger and Caty Wheelbarger, 10 Oct 1797.
John Stults and Madalana Caplinger, 11 Oct 1797.
William Mitchel and Eve Nestreete, 16 Oct 1797.
Henry Martin and Elisabeth Pitt, 25 Oct 1797.
Abraham Whitzel and Magdalin Keller, 5 Nov 1797.
Chrisley Beamand and Ann Ewbler, 7 Nov 1797.
Joseph Aldorphats and Margaret Seevely, 9 Nov 1797.
George Brunk and Nelly McCue, 9 Nov 1797.
John McKee and Jenny Berry, 9 Nov 1797.
Even Reece and Charlotte Mae, 20 Nov 1797.
Philip Spitzer and Eve Holsinger, 21 Nov 1797.
Edwin Nichols and Elizabeth Kring, 21 Nov 1797.
William Woods and Ruth Beazer, 25 Nov 1797.
John Harrison and Ann Tallman, 25 Nov 1797.
Thomas Campbell and Ann Blain, 2 Dec 1797.
Clemens Ewin and Jane Stuart, 5 Dec 1797.
William Smith and Dianna McDonough, 19 Dec 1797.
William Dunnavan and Keaty Gay, 20 Dec 1797.
John Saylor and Betsey Kysor, 26 Dec 1797.

Martin Buck and Mary Smith, 31 Dec 1797.
John Cole and Keaty Wolfe, 1 Jan 1798.
Robert Huston and Sarah Herron, 8 Jan 1798.
George Summers and Elizabeth Haney, 18 Jan 1798.
Jacob Fillinger and Elizabeth Sanger, 28 Jan 1798.
John Leonard and Sophia Krim, 29 Jan 1798.
Daniel Bowman and Ceny Zimmerman, 8 Feb 1798.
Jacob Wyant and Mary Gay, 9 Feb 1798.
Jacob Fox and Mary Ashenfelter, 17 Feb 1798.
Joseph Yunt and Elizabeth Bowman, 23 Feb 1798.
David Fisher and Rachel Peters, 26 Feb 1798.
Jacob Everheart and Keaty Stagleather, 9 April 1798.
John Shumaker and Barbara Countraman, 10 April 1798.
George Wolfe and Catharine Armontrout, 16 April 1798.
John Birer and Elizabeth Bowman, 17 April 1798.
John Kysor and Peggy Null, 23 April 1798.
Peter Staman and Madalena Swich, 23 April 1798.
Phillip Miller and Cloe Boshong, 24 April 1798.
John Roller and Susanna Wheelberger, 26 April 1798.
Jacob Harshbrger and Barbara Boshong, 15 May 1798.
Edward Ervin and Polly Stuart, 22 May 1798.
Martin Crotzsinger and Elizabeth Snider, 22 May 1798.
Mickeal Kline and Elisebeth Byrer, 22 May 1798.
Philip Deeds and Mary Bush, 25 May 1798.
Michael Kline and Elizabeth Byer, 2 June 1798.
Jacob Roop and Martha Price, 12 June 1798.
John Long and Elizabeth Comer, 12 June 1798.
Jacob Perky and Elizabeth Lemon, 25 June 1798.
Henry May and Keaty Sites, 25 June 1798.
Joseph Garver and Catharina Leedy, 26 June 1798.
Joseph Garvens and Catharine Lady, 24 July 1798.
William Michael and Keaty Louck, 26 July 1798.
John Brown and Magdalena Andis, 2 Aug 1798.
Martin Grimsley and Mary Strickler, 20 Aug 1798.
Abraham Haynes and Aseneth Rose, 25 Aug 1798.
Wm. Read and Elizabeth Snodden, 26 Aug 1798.

INDEX to Early Church Records of Rockingham County, Virginia

BOWEN, Amelia, 65
  Bro., 67
  Brother, 66
  Francis, 65
  Henry, 70
  Susanah, 82, 88
BOWER, John, 89
BOWERS, Elizabeth, 89
BOWGER, Polly, 88
BOWLAND, Mary, 87
BOWMAN, Augustine, 88
  Daniel, 90
  Elizabeth, 90
  John, 87
  Susanna, 86
BOYER (Beyer), Barbery, 77
  Eva, 19, 21
  John, 19, 21
  John George, 21
  Mary Margaret, 19
BOYLES, James, 86
BRABER..., ---, 57
BRACKEN, Rebecaha, 80
BRADSHAW, Elisabeth, 76
BRANEMAN, Ann, 72
BRANERMAN, Daniel, 74
BRANHAM, Sally, 71
  Sarah, 70
BRANN, Christina, 49
  Petter, 49
BRANNAM, Sary, 69
BRAUN, (D,X?)ebeda, 54
  Barbara, 36, 53
  Elisabeth, 35, 36, 37, 42, 54
  Georg, 53
  Margreth, 35
  Peter, 31, 35, 36, 37, 42, 54
BRAUN(IN), Magdalena, 10
  Maria, 9
BRAUNN, Jodel, 54
  Johannes, 54
BRAUT, Heinrich, 48
BREISS (Price), Augustin, 16
  Elisabeth, 16
BREIT, Anna, 57
  Carrolina, 57
  Charlot, 57
  Cohlman, 57
  Dalila Rigney, 57
  Druesilla, 57
  Jacob, 57
  Janeany, 57
  Johanes, 57
  Kinirmer, 57

Marshal, 57
BRENNER, Caspar, 1
  Casper, 1, 2, 6, 7, 9
  Catherina, 1, 4, 7, 8, 9
  Catherine, 1
  Christina, 9
  Johannes, 1
  John, 1
  Master, 10
  Michael, 9
  Sara, 1
BRETZS, John, 18
BRIG, Ruth, 67
BRIGHT (Brett), Anna Margaret, 20
  Catherine, 20
  John, 20
BRIGS, Ruth, 65
BRILIAN?/BRITIAN?, Christenah,
  74
BRILL, ---, 27
  Anna Maria, 28
  Thomas, 27, 28, 29, 86
BRIM, William, 72
BRISCH, Conrad, 19
  Elisabeth, 19
  Michael, 19
BRITAN, Mary, 82
BRITEN, Margret, 72
BRITON, ---, 67
  Margaret, 67
BRITTON, Lidea, 78
BROCH, Catharina, 52
BROCK, Polly, 87
BRODBECK, Susanna, 14
BRONNER, Caspar, 7
  Catherina, 7
BROOS, Hannes, 49
  Magdalena, 49
BROS, Christina, 43
  Elisabeth, 43
  Johanes, 43
BROSS, Elisabeth, 53
  Johanes, 40
  Johannes, 48
  Joseph, 53
  Sara, 53
  Stromor, 48
BROWN, John, 90
BRUMFIELD, David, 64
  Patience, 64
  Sister, 67
BRUMMER, Catharine, 17
  Peter, 17
BRUNK, Danel, 88

Frederick, 27
Margaret, 27
Valentin, 27
ERNSBERGER, Anna Maria, 34
Heinrich, 34, 35
Henrich, 35
Jacob, 35
Karl, 35
ERNST, Annamaria, 49
Georg, 49
ERVIN, Edward, 90
James, 86
Nancy, 86
Robart, 80
ERWIN, John, 78
Mary, 86, 87
Sarah, 86
ESTEL, Abigal, 74
Walis, 75
ESTELE, Ruth, 81
ESTELL, Samuel, 78
ESTERLE, Anna Maria, 4, 6
Casper, 6
Catherina, 6
Georg, 4, 6, 7, 9, 10
Magdalena, 6
Maria, 7
Moses, 6
ESTHEL, Fanny, 76
ETEIS, Catherina, 55
Johan, 55
EVANS, Thomas, 61, 62, 63
EVENS, Sidny, 76
William, 74
EVERHEART, Jacob, 90
EVINS, Griffith, 82
EVISON, Mary, 75
EWBLER, Ann, 89
EWENS, Sidny, 76
EWI, Anna, 8
Anna Maria, 8
Heinrich, 8
Margaretha, 8
Peter, 8
EWIN, Clemens, 89
Mary, 88
Sarah, 87
EWING, Aron, 82
EWINS, John, 75
EYHOLE, Adam, 82
EYLER, Catherine, 29
Peter, 29

-F-

FAIRBEARN, Robert, 88
FAIRS, Mary Ann, 77
FALUERS, ---, 27
Adam, 27
Maria, 27
FARLO, Edward, 82
FARQUER, David, 88
FATTORF, Johanes, 40
Sarah, 40
FAUSTER, Enoch, 84
James, 83
John, 81
FE....., Anna, 54
Jodrel, 54
FEAMSTER, Thomas, 84
FEGANS, Phillip, 61
FENCHEL, Friedrich, 53
Johannes, 53
Magdalena, 53
FENTER, Bedford, 83
FENTON, John, 77
FEY, Abraham, 24
Charles, 17
Dorothy, 17
John, 24
Susanna, 24
FICHER, Abraham, 40
FICKNER, Frederick, 87
FIELDS, Zachariah, 86
FIFER, Adam, 84
John, 70
FILLINGER, Elisabeth, 53
Heinrich, 53
Jacob, 53, 90
FINDER, Barbara, 17
Martin, 17
FINE, Grace, 66
FINKLE, Elizabeth, 87
FINN, Daniel, 87
FISCHBORN (Fishburn), Anna
Catherine, 18
Philip, 18
FISHER, David, 90
Isaac, 78
FLECHER, Phebe, 69
FLEMING, James, 80
Mary, 74, 81
Nancy, 80
FLEMINGS, Jane, 75
FLEMMEN, Matte, 78
FLESHMAN, Susanah, 84
FLETCHER, Sister, 71
FLIN, John, 84
FLINN, Polly, 82

GIESE, Frederick Henry, 21
GILASPY, Elisabeth, 77
GILKASON, James, 79
  John, 75
  Sarah, 75
GILLINER, William, 77
GINNUS, Georg, 52
  Magdalena, 52
GIVIN, Nancey, 84
GLASS, Mary, 76
GOAND, Edward, 81
GOAT, Elisabeth, 54
  Gad., 54
  Herichs Catherina, 54
GOOD, Peter, 69, 70
GORDAN, Charles, 70
GORDEN, Charles, 71
GORDON, Nancey, 69
  Nancy, 71
GOTTEL?/COTTEL?, Elisabeth, 75
GRABIEL, George, 68
GRACE, Magreat, 88
GRAEH, Catherina, 47
  Joh., 47
  Magdalena, 47
GRAEYE, Adam, 39
  Chatrina, 39
  Elisabeth, 39
  Jacob, 40
  Johan, 39
  Jonas, 39
GRAGG, Elesebeth, 87
GRAHAM, Duncan, 82
  Duncen, 82
  John, 87
GRAVES, Absalom, 66
GRAY, Margat, 78
  Tacey, 84
GREEN, Ann, 78
  Ezekiel, 86
  Henry, 80
  Jane, 87
  John, 88
  Margaret, 87
  Nancy, 86
GREVES, John, 84
GRIFF, Sussan, 75
GRIFFIN, Gordan, 76
  Isbill, 76
GRIFFITH, Benjamin, 58
  Elisabeth, 81
  James, 84
  Margarat, 84
GRIFFITS, William, 82

GRIGER, Barbra, 53
  Georg, 53
  Stuf, 53
GRIM, Johannes, 6
  Juliana, 6
  Peter, 6
  Sara, 6
GRIMSLEY, Martin, 90
GRODIN, Charles, 71
GROOS, Benjamin, 88
GROVES, John, 84
GRUB, Barbara, 17
  Daniel, 16
  Elisabeth, 16
  Jacob, 17
  Mary Catharine, 16
GUINN, Johnston, 87
GULLETT, Polly, 83
GULLY, Fransinah, 76
  Levine, 79
GUM, Elener, 65
  Mary, 88
  Norton, 65
GURRAT, Margrat, 76
GUT, Catherina, 5, 9
  Daniel, 9
  Heinrich, 5, 8
  Jacob, 9
  Margaretha, 9
GUTH, Heinrich, 8, 9
  Jacob, 9
  Margaretha, 9
  Philip, 9
GUTHMANN, Jacob, 29
GYATES, Ralph, 79

-H-
HABERSTICK, Adam, 2
  Elisabetha, 2
HAD, Georg, 49
  Johannes, 49
HAELLUENGER, Annamarie, 49
  Jacob, 49
HAHN, Mathaus, 9
HAIL, Elisabeth, 82
HAIN, Eva Elisabeth, 26
  Jonas, 26
HAISMAN, Elisabeth, 54
  Jacob, 54
HALL, James, 73, 74
  John, 87
HALLS, Nancy, 71
HAMAN, Phillip, 76
HAMANN, Elisabeth, 20

HUNDLY?/HANDLY?, Margreat, 74
HUNTER, Isbel, 82
HUSTON, Euphamis, 77
  Robert, 90
  Sarah, 78
HUTCHESON, John, 77
  Rhobaka, 77
HUTCHISON, Janey, 82
HUTTELLOCH, Andreas, 31
  Chatrina, 32
  Elisabeth, 42
  Jacob, 42
  Johan, 42
HUTTLOCH, Elisabeth, 46
  Johannes, 46
  Susanna, 46

-I-

IBBET, Ann, 74
IFRICH, Elisabeth, 55
  Georg, 55
IMAN, Daniel, 56
INGELS, Samual, 85
INGRAM, Nancy, 81
IRELAND, James, 64, 67

-J-

JACKMAN, John, 74
JACKSON, George Charles, 22
  Margaret, 22
  Mary, 88
  Robert, 88
  Sarah, 22
  William, 22
JACOBIN, Annmary, 74
JACOCKE, David, 83
JAMASON, James, 74
JAMES, Ann, 76
JAMISON, David, 77
  Samuel, 76
JANCKE, Jacob, 7
JARRATT, Jessie, 75
JARROT, Oen, 76
JAVEN, Danial, 82
JEFFERS, William, 77
JEFFREYS, ---, 67
  Rhoda, 67
JEFFRIES, Elisabeth, 80
JEMSON, Marget, 78
JENKINS, Ezkial, 82
JOHNSON, Jane, 78
  Margret, 78
  Polly, 87
  Robart, 78

Susanah, 77
JOHNSTON, Benjamin, 78
  Br., 67
  Brother, 65
  James, 64, 65
  Margrat, 82
  Mary, 80
  Robart, 80
  William, 81
JOHNSTUN, Margrat, 82
JONES, Ambrus, 79
  Danial, 82
  William, 80
JORDAN, John, 83
JOSEPH, Michall, 87
JULIUS, ---, 18
  Jacob, 18
JUTZLER, Elisabeth, 49
  Heinrich, 49

-K-

KARTH, Abraham, 47
  Dorothea, 47
  Franz, 47
KAB..., Peter, 54
KAUL, Anna Barbara, 22
  Christian, 22
  William, 22
KAUSH, Chatrina, 35
  Johan, 35
  Maria Madlena, 35
KAVANAUGH, Jael, 78
KEANY, John, 77
KEEFER, J., 57
KEEN, John, 85
  Neomia, 85
  Noomia, 85
KEENANY, Nelly, 75
KEENEY, Michel, 76
KEENY, David, 81
KEHRBACH, Anna, 40
  Georg, 40, 50
  Jacob, 50
  Sarah, 40
  Ziristinge, 40
KEIPF, Catherina, 7
  Michael, 7
KELLER, Anna Catherina, 45
  Catherina, 53
  Elisabeth, 53
  George, 29
  Gertraut, 45, 48
  Jacob, 39
  Johannes, 53

Michael, 4, 17
Noah, 4
Valentin, 4, 9
TRIBIG, Johannes Jost, 9
TRIMBEL, William, 81
TRIMBLE, Dvaid, 77
  Thomas, 80
TRORBACH, Barbara, 37
  Catherina, 46
  Chatrina, 32, 37
  Johan Heinrich, 32
  Wilhelm, 32, 37, 38
  William, 46
TRUCKWELL, Nansy, 77
TRUMBO, Dorotha, 89
  Jacob, 88
TUCKWELL, Nansy, 77
TUFERWEILER, Katherina, 52
TURPEN, Aaron, 80
  Martin, 80
  Moses, 77
TURPIN, Solomon, 81
TWITWILER, John, 88
TYRIE, William, 74

-U-

UNRUH, Elisabeth, 40, 45
UTERBOR, Christina, 54
  Johannes, 54

-V-

VAN GEMUENDEN, M.A., 13
VAN GENUENDEN, I.C., 13
VANCE, John, 87
  William, 74
VANORDAL, Laney, 84
VAUGHEB, Peggy, 84
VAZ, Anna Maria, 34
  Jacob, 34
  Johanes, 34
VENBEBBER, Eleaner, 80
  Peter, 80
  Verona, 78
VENDEVORTER?/
    VENDWARTER/
    VENDEVERTER?, Jacob, 74
VENUS, Abraham, 37
  Anna Margaret, 20
  Christian, 33
  Christoph, 37, 42
  Henry, 20
  Margaret, 20
  Maria, 33, 37
  Maria Barbara, 42

VINCEN, Sarah, 83
  Susanah, 83
VINCON, Sarah, 83
  Susanah, 83
VINCY, Dinah, 84
  Sarah, 84
VINE, Hannah, 83
VINEY, Dinah, 84
  Hannah, 83
  Leah, 81
  Rachel, 80
  Sarah, 84
VINSON, Sarah, 71
VOGT, Caspar, 14
  Catharine, 15
  Catharine Margaret, 15
  Elisabeth, 12, 15
  Elizabeth, 14, 30
  John Caspar, 12, 15
  Martin, 30
  Sarah, 12
VOLLMER, Ludwig, 10
VOLMER, Ludwig, 5
VOTSCH, Catharine, 15
  John, 15

-W-

WAGENER (Waggoner), George, 27
  Jacob, 27
WAGNER, Elisabetha, 2
  Elizabeth, 25
  Georg, 2
  George, 24, 25, 30

  Jacob, 2
  John, 25
  John George, 24
WAHL, Conrad, 11
WALKER, James, 79
  Maryann, 84
WALLIS, John, 76
  Margrat, 84
WALTHER, Elisabetha, 3
  Noah, 3
  Thomas, 3
WARD, Jane, 82
  Kezia, 79
  Rhobacah, 76
WAREN, Catherine, 63
  Eleoner, 87
  Michael, 87
  Timothy, 63
WARING, Hannah, 74
WARREN, Sarah, 73

www.ingramcontent.com/pod-product-compliance
Lightning Source LLC
Chambersburg PA
CBHW071134280326
41935CB00010B/1223